ECHO OF JESUS' PRAYER

- IN THE CHURCH

Jesus Christ's Intentions for Humanity through the Church

MARTIN S. MANUEL

First Edition

Website: www.echoofjesusprayer.org
E-mail: PrintBook1@echoofjesusprayer.org

ISBN: 978-0692779842 (Martin S. Manuel)

In memory of my beloved parents:
James W. (Jinx) and Florine E. (Flo) Manuel

Contents

Preface

Florine, my mother, celebrated her 90th birthday with over 100 of her offspring—fifteen biological children, one adopted child, dozens of grandchildren, as many great-grandchildren, and even some great-great-grandchildren. Often she reflected on her large family, some enjoying upper-middle-class living standards, others struggling to keep their homes, most maintaining relatively good health, one or two hardly as healthy as she, several unable to get along with each other, all deeply dwelling in the middle of her heart where her foremost desire was always for their wellness and happiness.

Mom gave birth to seventeen children—nine male and eight female—all through Dad, her husband of nearly fifty years. Despite having the same parents, we the children do not all look alike. Our diverse looks depict the diversity of our personalities, our temperaments, our strengths, our weaknesses, our talents, and our birth-order effects. These dissimilarities contribute additively to what at times comes across as violent disagreements on matters that, in most cases, all of us agree are of utmost importance, matters that included proper care of our parents.

Our family is a microcosm of the family of believers of Jesus Christ—the Church, having a strong bond of common faith, yet driven to deep divisions in beliefs and relationships.

Seeing a matter from a personal point of view tends to heighten its reality. For that reason, I have chosen to illustrate here the dilemma of family disunity from the eyes of a human parent, an illustration that can help us to see the dilemma of Church disunity from the eyes of the perfectly-one God: Father, Son, and Spirit.

Is Church oneness, or "unity" as translated in Ephesians 4:3, important to God?

As parents of two adult children, my wife and I have winced each time that they argued, fought, or acted resentfully toward each other. My dad enforced strictly his rule against fighting, as if it was the most important of all his rules for his children, pulling out his belt to whack the back sides of any of us who violated the rule; I am an experienced witness. It is important to us parents.

Is it important to God?

As a pastor, one of my deepest disappointments was to witness infighting in congregations that I had been blessed to serve. It was in the midst of one such incident that the inspiration of Jesus' prayer recorded in John 17 occurred to me, becoming the text of a series of sermons and afterward the theme scripture of my Masters' thesis.

Oneness was so important to Jesus that it was one of the major themes of his prayer with and for his disciples shortly before he went to the Garden of Gethsemane where he was betrayed. When something is one's last prayer, be sure that it is of utmost importance and highest priority. This book is about that prayer of Jesus. My intent is to clearly present his prayer, explaining the astonishing background behind it, emphasizing the significance of oneness, elaborating on the weight he placed on it, stating the amazing impact he predicted oneness would bring, highlighting its strategic importance in the purpose of God. My hope and prayer is that we—Jesus' followers—get it, deeply understanding the oneness imparted by the Spirit, realizing that keeping it is our charge, making every effort to pursue it in one-on-one, group-to-group, and all other levels of relationships.

This book uses the word "oneness" extensively. The word does not appear in most English Bibles, but "one" appears in the text that I chose, John 17. The Greek words ἑν [*hen*] and εἰς [*heis*] are translated "one" in English. Other texts that I will address, Ephesians 4:3 and 13, translate ἑνοτητα [*henotēta*] "unity" from this same root.[1] Various authors quoted in this book

---

[1] Archibald T. Robertson, *Word Pictures in the New Testament* (Nashville, TN: Broadman Press, 1933), Logos Software 4 on Eph. 4:2. "**The unity** (την ἑνοτητα [*tēn henotēta*]). Late and rare word (from εἰς [*heis*], one), in Aristotle and Plutarch, though in N. T. only here and verse 13."

use the words oneness, unity, and union interchangeably in similar contexts. I prefer oneness, but I leave their choices of terms in quotes unchanged.

The term oneness might be confused with "oneness theology" of Unitarians or Unitarianism. The biblical concept of oneness as discussed in this book has nothing to do with these ideas. Unitarianism is described as: "The doctrinal system characterized chiefly by belief in the unipersonality of God and the normal humanity of Jesus, as contrasted with the Trinity and the eternal deity of Christ."[2] Neither does this book have anything to do with "Oneness Theology" or "Oneness Pentecostalism"—more widely known as "Modalism," which hold: "the one God appeared in three distinct 'modes' or 'manifestations'—as Father in creation, as the Son in redemption, and as the Holy Spirit in regeneration."[3] As we shall see, the very word that Jesus spoke translated one in English necessitates more than one person.

In endeavoring to understand Jesus' use of this term, oneness, applying it to his followers—the church, I will start with a basic question: In the first place, what good is the church? Why is it so important that Jesus prayed that it would be one, and what is the relevance of the church to us? Next I will discuss Jesus, his love, his revelation of God's love, and his prayer for his followers in the first century, and as he clearly stated, his followers afterward, who became the church through all ages—that they would be one. Then I will briefly examine church history to see successful fulfillment of as well as notable failure to fulfill Jesus' prayer. Finally, I will explore biblical examples and propose ways by which Jesus' followers can and will echo Jesus' prayer.

---

[2] Vergilius Ferm, ed., *The Encyclopedia of Religion* (Secaucus, NJ: Poplar Book, 1945), 801.

[3] Thabiti M. Anyabwile, *The Decline of African American Theology* (Downers Grove, IL: InterVarsity Press, 2007), 95.

-1-
What Good is Church?

Church: I recall my first impression at six years old, dressed in new clothes, walking with my three older siblings, passing by a church building, asking why we can't go there, fatigued after a half mile, finally arriving to experience something I couldn't possibly understand, knowing only that my nose was running and I didn't have a handkerchief. What good was it?

Attendance as a pre-teen was not a habit, but about the time that I became a teenager, something stirred my mom to insist that her kids start back attending church, at least while she was so motivated, which went on for a few years. To me, nothing seemed more irrelevant: chants and songs in Latin, none making sense, incense permeating the air within, darkening the already-dimly-lit sanctuary, irritating my nostrils, stimulating my runny nose with such a flow that the tissues I brought soon began to crumble. No way out of the tightly-packed pews, until the mass ended I was trapped, like a car stuck in the mud. Whenever I could avoid attendance, I did, even at the risk of disappointing my mom.

My viewpoint as a teen was much like many today, seeing in church no relevancy to life, feeling extreme discomfort in church settings, having no reason to be part of a church, wondering why anyone else would. In a 2014 study[4] of over 4000 Americans across the country by the Barna Group, half (49%) surveyed said that church was "somewhat" or "very important" while the other half (51%) said that it was "not too" or "not at all important." Of the latter group, the question was asked, "Why don't you attend church?" According to the survey results, "Across age and

---

[4] Barna Group, *Americans Divided on the Importance of Church*, March 2014, Barna Group, The Importance of Church.pdf.

denomination, the top two reasons unchurched Americans said they didn't think attending church was important were always the same:" 40% said "I find God elsewhere;" 35% said, "Church is not relevant to me personally."

My viewpoint agreed with those in the 35% of-the-unchurched-group. I was carefree, experiencing secure living with my parents and siblings, enjoying the basic essentials—food, clothing, shelter—having good health and the vigor of youth, living in the freedom and opulence typical of average Americans, seeing nothing in church that I needed.

The group that said they find God elsewhere likely belonged to another religion or perhaps were among those who consider themselves spiritual and not in need of a group to access God. I will address their sentiment later in this chapter.

Among the half that consider church important, megachurches—churches whose attendance numbers run in the thousands—have a growing proportion of attendees. A 2015 study[5] with results reported in the *Christian Post* found that "general attendance numbers in a strong majority of megachurches are growing," nonetheless, the research also found that "weekly megachurch attendance numbers are dropping"—more members attending less regularly.

Disagreement prevails, and even where there is belief in the relevancy of church, that belief is accompanied by decreased involvement. The vital question is who is correct? If those who see no relevance in church are right, the others are hanging on to an unrealistic hope. On the other hand, if those who see relevance in church are correct, the others are missing something of utmost importance. Can Americans simply agree to disagree? Of course! Yet that would be similar to two groups journeying through a cave with two paths but only one way out. The half that chooses the incorrect path is in trouble!

I was in that group throughout my primary and secondary school years. Then suddenly, my viewpoint started to change

[5] Samuel Smith, *Megachurches Seeing Drop in Weekly Attendance, Study Finds*, Christian Post, December 3, 2015.

when at eighteen, I went through a scary life-changing experience that led me to ask the big question: what relevancy is God? At the time it seemed that there was no relationship between God and what I knew as church. Eventually I saw otherwise, evidenced by this topic.

What changed? Consider the first four words of this book's title: *Echo of Jesus' Prayer*, the subject of which is Jesus, not church. Like many others, even when I knew little about religion, I held Jesus in higher regard than the church, recalling stories about his love, suspecting that there was something truly special about him, all along, though, only marginally interested. Nonetheless, when I perceived a connection between Jesus and my hope to keep on living, the possibility grabbed my attention enough to motivate me to look deeper. What I saw launched me into a pursuit that hasn't abated. So when, where, and how did the church enter the picture? I will not attempt to answer that question until a little later in this chapter. First I'd like to revisit my childhood of dislike of the church, because I had missed something.

Much later in my adulthood I looked back and realized that Mom's church was not completely irrelevant. Back then in our small Midwest town, my dad, along with thousands of other workers, had lost his job when a publishing company of a major national magazine closed. Without sufficient income to pay living expenses, my parents accepted charity, weekly donations of bread and milk through the church's nun convent.

Each week, the nuns gave our family vouchers to take to nearby bakery and dairy stores to receive, without charge, enough loaves of bread and jars of milk to feed, together with other groceries, a family of eleven children along with our two parents. Mom would send two or three of us boys, who were big enough to go on our own, to the stores. Without considering the source of these necessities, I was sustained, along with all my family, for more than a year through this charitable act until our dad found suitable work. This good deed did not register in my mind as provision through the grace of God. In retrospect, I now understand that good lay beneath the archaic traditions of Mom's church and non-reputable acts of some church members.

However, charity alone does not constitute relevance, and anyway, churches have no corner on charity. So, back to the question, what relevance is the church? The answer is simple: none, unless Jesus is who he claimed to be, and he is in the Church, making it relevant. If Jesus is not in the Church, the Church is worthless, an invention of the superstitious, a vessel of opportunists, a masquerade for any real relevancy. Let me restate with emphasis: **Unless Jesus gives it worth, the Church is worthless!**

What is the Church?

You may have noticed that in the previous paragraph I capitalized the initial C in Church. I did so deliberately. The New Testament books originally were written in Greek. The English word church is translated from the Greek word ἐκκλησιαν [*ekklēsian*],[6] first used in the New Testament in Jesus' statement in Matthew 16:18, "I will build my church." The word generally means assembly and was so used in Deuteronomy 10:4 of the Septuagint, a Greek translation of the original Hebrew. The New Testament writers extensively used it for the whole group of Christians (1 Corinthians 12:28) and for local congregations (Acts 15:41).

My use of "Church" pertains to the whole group of Christians without the various identifiers in their names that distinguish one organization or group from another. Let me use an illustration to clarify. "Dog" is the designation of a four-legged animal that has

---

[6] Archibald T. Robertson, *Word Pictures in the New Testament* (Nashville, TN: Broadman Press, 1933), Logos Software 4 on Mat. 16:18. "It is the figure of a building and he uses the word ἐκκλησιαν [*ekklēsian*] which occurs in the New Testament usually of a local organization, but sometimes in a more general sense. What is the sense here in which Jesus uses it? The word originally meant "assembly" (Acts 19:39), but it came to be applied to an "unassembled assembly" as in Acts 8:3 for the Christians persecuted by Saul from house to house. "And the name for the new Israel, ἐκκλησια [*ekklēsia*], in His mouth is not an anachronism. It is an old familiar name for the congregation of Israel found in Deut. (18:16; 23:2) and Psalms (22:3–6), both books well known to Jesus" (Bruce).

canine teeth and usually is domesticated, but the word can apply to a despicable person or one that is considered lucky. In the same way that "dog" can have different meanings, "church" can apply to organizations that may or may not resemble the intentions of the New Testament writers.

When Jesus said, "I will build **my** church," he had something specific in mind, not just any assembly of people, not just a local congregation or denomination, but an entity that would belong to him. Paul referred to Jesus as "head of the body, the church," (Colossians 1:18) and he added that "there is one body" (Ephesians 4:4). Into this one body all Church members are baptized (1 Corinthians 12:13), and their names are enrolled in heaven (Hebrews 12:23), whether or not they are listed on a church roll of some earthly organization. It is this one Church that I am addressing. Thus, the Church is a body of spiritually-baptized members, a body that Jesus heads and owns, and a body whose membership is established in heaven.

Some of the various church groups claim that they are the true church and either assert or imply that only they can claim that distinction. On the basis of the biblical insistence that there is one body or Church, and all believers in Jesus Christ are baptized into that one body, and that the names of these members are enrolled in heaven, I challenge that claim. I challenge it on the authority of Peter's inspired answer to those who asked him, "What shall we do [to be saved]?" His answer was not, join this or that church. It was "Repent and be baptized, every one of you, in the name of Jesus Christ for the forgiveness of your sins" (Acts 2:37-38). Jesus saves people (Matthew 1:21; Acts 4:12; 10:43) and immerses them into the Church through the Holy Spirit (Acts 11:16-17). Repentance and belief in Jesus, confirmed by baptism, constitutes the acceptance of the free gift of salvation. No organization can claim that which alone belongs to Jesus Christ. As Peter, speaker of the words Luke quoted in Acts 11, was surprised when Jesus baptized believing Gentiles with the Holy Spirit, can Jesus' servants today admit with humility that they too do not determine who Jesus decides to save?

The Italians who believed Peter were enrolled in heaven, baptized with the Holy Spirit into the one body—the Church, the same Church into which Jewish believers were baptized (Acts 11:18; 1 Corinthians 12:13). The New Testament writers, especially Luke, discussed this Church, telling the story of its inception and growth in the book of Acts, spanning a period of about 30 years. When the 27 books of the New Testament were canonized late in the second century,[7] there was only one Church with many congregations spread across the Middle East, Northern Africa, Europe, and parts of Asia. Early Christian leaders, such as Irenaeus of Lyons, wrote extensively about heresy plaguing the Church in the second century: heretics, not different churches, were the problem. Out of these and other heresies, over time, various groups emerged, tiny in comparison to the whole, ultimately becoming either geographically isolated or extinct.

The first major division in church history occurred in 1054 AD, when leaders from Constantinople of the Eastern churches and leaders from Rome of the Western churches clashed over the wording of the Nicene Creed issued in 381 AD. Each division resulted in identifiers by name that distinguished one from another: Orthodox church, Roman Catholic church, out of which later came the Church of England—Anglican and Episcopal. Since then, most divisions have come out of the Western church, especially those that were the outcome of the Protestant Reformation in the sixteenth century and the plethora of divisions since in Protestantism. Each of these divisions generated new designations: Lutheran church, Reformed church, Presbyterian church, Methodist church, Baptist church, Adventist church, Pentecostal churches with names such as Church or Assembly of ____ (God, Christ, you name it). These are only some of the far-too-many-to-name groups that claim the designation church.

In some cases, different designations were inevitable. Where geographical, language, cultural, and national barriers made unity

---

[7] Robert W. Jenson, *Canon and Creed,* Louisville, KY: Westminster John Knox Press, 2010. Jensen believes that the NT canon was "functional in the latter part of the second century" (*Ch. 1*).

difficult, distinctive names became a necessity. Such is the case in the Orthodox churches, where the national or language distinction became part of the designation: Greek Orthodox and Russian Orthodox.

In most cases, different designations arose out of disputes and disagreements about doctrine or procedure. The more radical of these are found in the Western church, and division is rampant in Protestantism, especially in the United States.

I do not consider what I am calling the Church to be any particular one of the entities that have emerged out of the various divisions. In this book, what I am calling the Church stands above all of these. Members of the Church **include** members of the many groups that are designated church, but **not all** individuals or groups so designated are part of the Church that Hebrews 12:23 says consists of names enrolled in heaven. The distinguishing factor is that Jesus is in the Church and head of it. Paul wrote about this Church in Ephesians 5:25-27 as the bride of Jesus:

> Christ loved the church and gave himself up for her to make her holy, cleansing her by the washing with water through the word, and to present her to himself as a radiant church, without stain or wrinkle or any other blemish, but holy and blameless.

Someone might say, "That's it! That's the kind of church that I would respect!" Paul's portrayal of a church as a perfectly-flawless, beautiful woman does not look like what we see in any of the different groups called church. Why?

Under Construction

Jesus spoke of building the Church. As explained above, it is an assembly of people that Jesus said he would build. What did he mean by that? Peter's first epistle helps to explain, writing in metaphorical language about Jesus' construction project: "You also, like living stones, are being built into a spiritual house" (1 Peter 2:5). Peter depicted the Church as **being** built. Paul used the same metaphor in one of his letters: "The whole building is joined together and rises to become a holy temple in the Lord" (Ephesians 2:21). Paul said the building is **rising**. Both apostles considered the Church a work in progress. No one looks at a building under construction and expects it to look finished. Yet, the misconception held by many people who notice imperfections in churches leads them to evaluate the churches as if they were finished products.

After being married three and one half years, my wife and I decided that it was time to purchase a home, having outgrown our two-bedroom apartment after the birth of our second child. The nice thing about that apartment was that the building was quite new and modern. We wanted the same feel in our home along with more space, but after the realtor learned what we could afford in mortgage payments, modern and new were out. We settled for an old bungalow—a "fixer upper." When remodeling began, the quaint little house became messy. As we painted ceilings and walls and added new fixtures, the house looked ugly, and it stayed that way until the new carpet was laid. If you have lived through remodeling, you understand; if not, visit a construction site. The metaphor of a building under construction portrays the ever-changing spiritual state of the Church, unavoidably messy, appearing to be ugly at times on both the exterior and interior, gradually moving toward completion each day, although the progress may be difficult to perceive.

The metaphor of a bride preparing for her wedding is similar: she is only finished when everything about her—head to toe, nails to makeup, teeth included—all is completely flawless. Paul had this in mind when he wrote about the "radiant church, without stain or wrinkle or any other blemish." A bride does not instantly become prepared; it takes time and diligence, and according to Paul's words, it is Christ himself who does the purification of his bride.

Still another metaphor depicts the life-journey of individual church members as growth (2 Peter 3:18), starting out as spiritual infants, eventually becoming spiritually grown up (1 Corinthians 3:1). These metaphors explain the sharp contrast between Jesus and the Church. The perfect Jesus Christ is head of the Church, which consists of imperfect people, weak in face of temptation, naturally inclined to sin, making all kinds of mistakes and yet called saints (Romans 1:7; 2 Corinthians 1:1; Ephesians 1:1). They are distinguished from those not called saints in two ways: 1) their sins are forgiven, thus through Jesus they are holy, and 2) they are being transformed daily inwardly through the Holy Spirit so that they are becoming more like Jesus each day.

Paul's letter to the church at Rome extensively explains. Romans stands out among the epistles of the New Testament as an exposition of the Gospel—the good news—of Jesus Christ. Unlike the four Gospels, Romans does not present a biographical sketch of Jesus; instead, it explains the purpose, meaning, and outcome of the gospel.

In the early chapters of the letter, Paul explains why the good news of Jesus is necessary, showing that whether we consider the Gentiles with their philosophy or the Jews with their law-oriented religion, the picture is the same: colossal failure; indeed, Paul concludes, the whole human race has fallen and is doomed to destruction (Romans 1:18-3:20). The chapters that follow go on to show that in face of this calamity, God showed grace to humanity, out of love sending his perfect Son to atone for human sin and represent humanity, leading those who trust and follow Jesus to triumphant living now through the indwelling Holy Spirit and the hope of being resurrected into everlasting life (Romans 3:21-8:39).

With this explanation as the backdrop, Paul urges his readers to give themselves sacrificially to God and refrain from conformance with the way of this world in favor of being transformed by a process of renewal of their minds (Romans 12:1-2). He follows with a detailed description in the 12th

Chapter of what living as transformed people looks like. The following is a summary:

V. 3-8. In thought, the individual Christian is a small part of something much larger, each part living together like the cells of a healthy human body with each member or part contributing uniquely to the health and success of the whole.

V. 9-13. In living, the individual Christian sincerely loves, respects, and honors others; practicing a life of joyful hope in the promised future, enduring patiently inevitable present difficulties, praying everyday, and sharing with people in need.

V. 14-21. In relationships, the individual Christian blesses people, genuinely commiserates, sympathizes, strives for peace, and always tries to do the right thing toward others.

Now, someone might say, that's what I am looking for in the behavior of church people. Yes, but herein lays a problem. Many people expect others to live good lives without holding themselves to the same standard. While serving as a church pastor, I often heard complaints from a church member who had the amazing ability to diagnose the faults of everyone but herself. She would angrily shout, "We have to love each other," all the while behaving in a way that disrespected others and put her interests first. Of all the church members, only she incurred a criminal record after her baptism—not that the crime was a special problem; we all make mistakes; I mention that only in the context of her general misbehavior. She, like the Samaritan woman at the well (John 4:16-18), lived with a man who was not her husband, but unlike the Samaritan woman, she was not interested in having that fact brought to her attention. She would complain that she was tired of church and insisted that being in a relationship with Jesus was all that she needed, not realizing that her relationship with Jesus was actually expressed through her relationship with church members.

Paul's description of life in the Church shows that it is in the interaction with church members—humans with faults like our own—that we grow in conformance with Jesus (Philippians 2:3-5). By interacting with imperfect people, we learn humility, patience with others, forgiveness, and tolerance of differences. It is in the Church that spiritual growth takes place. In short, being in Church makes better church members, while living separately from the Church limits growth.

How does this spiritual transformation happen? Clearly, the transformation of a church member is **not** accomplished through human effort. Paul said, "be transformed" not transform yourself. In 2 Corinthians 3:17-18, he explains how it happens:

> Now the Lord is the Spirit, and where the Spirit of the Lord is, there is freedom. And we all, who with unveiled faces contemplate the Lord's glory, are being transformed into his image with ever-increasing glory, which comes from the Lord, who is the Spirit.

The Lord Jesus works through the Holy Spirit living within the church member to change gradually the human church member into the likeness of the human Jesus in character, while the member retains individuality as a person. The glory is within, not in a shining face, and it increases or grows steadily over the lifetime of the church member. As the growth of a plant can be so gradual that from one day to the next change is not discernable, so the church member's growth is gradual. At no time in the pre-resurrected life does he or she reach perfection, but when Jesus reappears, he dramatically completes the transformation of the church member, causing the raised body to be like his glorious body (Philippians 3:21), as living things give birth to new living things like them though smaller in comparison.

Jesus does the transformation work by his power through the Holy Spirit, but each church member is a participant in the process. That is why Paul wrote, "be transformed." It is with the willingness, cooperation, and earnest desire of the church member that Jesus does the work; otherwise, it would be forced. How does the church member participate? Paul answered in his words that immediately precede "be transformed"—"offer your bodies as living sacrifices" and "do not conform to... the world" (Romans 12:1-2). While the church member willingly yields to the transforming work within, he or she faces the resistance of conformity with everything that comes with being a broken, fallen, human in this broken and fallen world. In electrical components, resistance to flowing current can produce heat. Similarly, the heat or stress of this spiritual resistance results in the refinement of the person spiritually, similar to the way that precious metals are refined.

In addition to the resistance of broken humanity in a broken world, each church member, like every other human being, experiences personal troubles in the course of life. To the church member, personal troubles are proving ground of faith, the outcome of which is more spiritual refinement (1 Peter 1:6-7). In face of such troubles, the Church offers another benefit in the same way that support groups help their participants. Church members help each other through times of adversity, empathetically sharing in their troubles and participating with each other in prayer.

So if this refinement process is really happening, why is it not more evident in churches? Part of the answer is that not all churches and not all church members are participating. Studies of church attendance tell a story of declining interest in Christianity in America, but Ed Stetzer wrote in a CNN report that there is more to it than just the numbers. Stetzer defined Christians in the United States as belonging to three categories: cultural Christians, congregational Christians, and convictional Christians. He wrote:

> Cultural Christians are the least connected – they call themselves Christian because of heritage or culture. Congregational Christians have some connection to a local church, but rarely attend. On the other hand, convictional Christians call themselves Christian like the other two

categories, but they attend services regularly and order their lives around their faith convictions.[8]

Stetzer did not use the language of Romans 12 in these comments, but I think his point is the same. Two of the three types of Christians that he denotes are, by their level of involvement, not participating. However, those Stetzer called "convictional Christians" not only attend church services regularly, but live out their faith daily. In practice, they live sacrificially for Jesus and resist conformity to the world. Although the number of church members participating in Jesus' transformation and refinement process is much lower than the total number of Americans who claim to be church-goers, the Church continues today to be in, and headed by, Jesus Christ.

Another explanation for what may seem to be a lack of evidence that this refinement process is really happening in churches is the private nature of personal-inner transformation. It is discernable only through the fruit of good works, and as the example I mentioned before of the good works of my mom's church was to me unnoticed for many years, sometimes only a look back can see it. Even the Lord Jesus had his critics during his life, critics who believed that they saw evil in him, the perfect, sinless Son of God! Likewise, Paul had his critics, especially in Jerusalem, critics who not only overlooked his work among Gentiles but even considered it evil. In America during the civil-rights movement, many were the critics of Dr. Martin Luther King. Only later, when history portrayed a full picture of his work and its result, did appreciation for his contributions result in national recognition. Church members in whom Jesus is at work exhibit similar fruits in their lives, but at the same time they find their good work the subject of criticism by some. To those who experienced such criticism in the first century, Peter wrote in 1 Peter 2:12:

---

[8] Ed Stetzer, *No, American Christianity is not dead*, CNN, May 16, 2015.

> Live such good lives among the pagans that, though they accuse you of doing wrong, they may see your good deeds and glorify God on the day he visits.

Peter understood that as the saying goes, you can't win them all. Some things only become clear over time when prejudices, deliberate slander, and misunderstandings fade along with those who promote them; that's when the truth comes out. Peter's statement suggests that those who accuse often simply do not understand and will see things differently when Jesus returns.

To the same people, Peter wrote in 4:4 about another type of put-down experienced by church members: "They think it strange that you do not plunge with them into the same flood of dissipation, and they heap abuse on you."

Sometimes church members whose lives have been radically changed through their repentance and Jesus' inner transformation become the brunt of criticism from people who resent their new lifestyle, calling them names such as "goody-goody-two-shoes." Envy and feelings of inferiority in the critic are often the cause. In some cases, the church member may invite such remarks by falling into self-righteous attitudes toward others. Those in Christ may make this mistake, but, Jesus continues their transformation. In all of these instances, the critics are themselves loved by God, and his plan for them involves a positive witness by the Church even if it is not immediately understood or appreciated.

No Excuses

Nothing written thus far excuses the abuses, insults, persecutions, murders, and atrocities committed by churches or individual church members at any time in history.

From time to time, a news story tells about a pastor who commits criminal acts of abuse against children. Not as often reported are church leaders who abuse members through authoritarian practices. Some churches have promoted ideas that damaged family relationships and endangered the health of church members and their children—all under the guise of doing what pleases God.

Some churches have encouraged violent activism, resulting in attacks against people or institutions that are considered ungodly. Still other churches target certain individuals or groups for hateful condemnations. History tells of the Crusades, the Inquisitions, and of religiously-incited atrocities by professing Christians against other Christians, perceived pagans, or people considered infidels.

Christian individuals and institutions have fallen miserably short of the standards taught in the New Testament. Rest assured, Jesus **never** abused, insulted, murdered, or persecuted! The event in Jesus' life story that some may consider persecution—his ouster of the money changers from the temple court—did not involve an attack on a human or even an animal, unless one considers an overturned table an injury. Instead, Jesus taught the opposite of violence: Blessed are the peacemakers, turn the other cheek, love your enemies (Matthew 5:9, 39, 44).

Jesus warned his disciples that "a time is coming when anyone who kills you will think he is offering a service to God" (John 16:2). The Church was destined to suffer persecution, but persecution is not part of Christian behavior. The hundreds of pages in the New Testament offer no examples of, or instructions about, persecution by Christians or the Church against anyone. To anyone who has experienced persecution from the Church, I offer a sincere apology, and I know of many other Christians who agree and would do likewise. Such should **never** be the case. There is no valid reason to inflict harm in the name of religion.

Jesus intended the opposite for the Church, telling his followers that they were the salt of the earth and the light of the world (Matthew 5:13-16).

Jesus and the Church

This Chapter posed the question, what good is the Church? The answer, already asserted, is that it is worthless unless Jesus Christ is in it, heading it and giving it worth. As explained, Jesus said the Church belongs to him, his construction project, not yet completed—according to Peter and Paul—but being built. Paul took it a little further by saying that Jesus is the chief cornerstone (Ephesians 2:20). He is both builder of it and resident in it. Of all the institutions on earth: nations, governments, alliances, cities, corporations, religious organizations, other organizations, and every grouping of people, the Church alone bears this distinction. None else was founded by, overseen by, and indwelt by the glorified human Son of God.

Jesus did not stop when he said, "I will build my Church." Reading on in Matthew 16:18 we see that he added assurance that it would never die by saying, "and the gates of Hades will not overcome it."[9] Nearly two thousand years later, Jesus' assurance stands; the Church has not died.

Furthermore, Jesus showed, as Matthew recorded in 16:19, the Church is not only a unique institution on earth, but in it can be found "the keys of the kingdom of heaven." Imagine two houses, side by side, separated by a small yard on each property, with one house secured by a locked door. To access that house from the other, one must have keys to unlock the door. Jesus gave the keys of God's house to Peter, the leader of those who would become the Church; since then, the Church possesses these keys. Access to the kingdom of heaven starts with Jesus and goes through the Church.

Those who want to be in a spiritual relationship with Jesus but not part of what some term "an organized church" are missing the fact that Jesus is in the Church, thus those who have a spiritual relationship with Jesus are in it with him. Those who are drawn to Jesus, seeing in him something relevant, discover that Jesus has a place for them, along with everyone who shares the desire for a spiritual connection with him, and that place is the

---

[9] D. A. Carson, et al., ed., *New Bible Commentary: 21st Century Edition* (Leicester, England; Downers Grove, IL: Inter-Varsity Press, 1994, 4th ed.), 926. *"The gates of Hades* is a poetic expression for death; this new community of those who follow Jesus will never die".

Church. Why? The amazing answer is found in Jesus' prayer, which will be explored later.

Did Jesus make a mistake in placing such importance on the Church? Didn't he know that Peter and the other Apostles would make mistakes? Couldn't he see that eventually problems would plague this Church that he built? Of course he did, but remember, he is in it—long after Peter and the other apostles died—he is present to ensure that the Church continues to exist and fulfill its purpose. He is there, and with the Holy Spirit he is refining the Church, purifying it of its faults—even using those faults to facilitate the purification process. Only those who faithfully live in the Church, being transformed by the indwelling Holy Spirit, loving fellow members, forgiving offences, tolerating differences, resisting the evil influence of the world, experience spiritual refinement in action.

Now please consider this: who is served by the perception that the Church is irrelevant or no good? Who would discourage not only Jesus' followers but humanity from being involved where he is present? Who benefits when churches sink into irrelevancy through devaluing the importance of Jesus' presence, distracting church members from daily living out their faith, and elevating archaic practices above Jesus' intentions? If we understand that it is the enemy—of God and his people—who perpetrates these lies, will we gullibly believe them and shun the Church? To confront these lies so well disseminated that they permeate human culture, I chose as the title of this chapter a lying-suggestive question: *What good is church?*

Now, let's consider what we all know is good. We humans tend to respond with love when we are loved. From infanthood, we feel the love of mother and father, and in a short time, we began to respond to this love, smiling at our parents' smile, wanting to be held, and feeling insecure when they are not nearby. As we grow older, we learn to respond to friendly gestures from those who we did not know previously, making new friends. Even romantic attraction hinges on mutual attraction expressed in mutual love. Instinctively, humans want and need to love and be loved.

The 2015 science-fiction movie, *Interstellar*, curiously wove the matter of the human need for love into the need to survive and quest to explore. One of the movie's stars, scientist, Dr. Amelia Brand, while on a mission with other astrophysicists in a desperate attempt to save humanity, spoke these words, considered by some to be the crux of the movie:

> Love isn't something we invented. It's observable, powerful, it has to mean something... something we can't yet understand. Maybe it's some evidence, some artifact of a higher dimension that we can't consciously perceive. I'm drawn across the universe to someone I haven't seen in a decade, who I know is probably dead. Love is the one thing we're capable of perceiving that transcends dimensions of time and space. Maybe we should trust that, even if we can't understand it.

Not much to debate here. Science, philosophy, religion, and human reasoning all agree that love is good. Therefore, it is reasonable that the perception of not being loved repels people from church-goers. Using the same reasoning, will not people be drawn to genuine love from the Church? These questions will be explored in detail in Chapter 5.

Jesus, in contrast to church-goers, enjoys a reputation of being a special person. Even to those who regard him as a good man and a wonderful religious teacher and nothing more, consensus is that he believed in, taught, and practiced love. That reputation is not necessarily shared by the deities of other religions, leading to this question, what is it about Jesus that draws people to him? Jesus' chilling answer to this question is: "But I, when I am lifted up from the earth, will draw all men to myself" (John 12:32). Being lifted up is an allusion to his crucifixion.

During his earthly ministry, crowds were drawn to him because of the miracles, but only a small percentage of the crowds became his followers. Jesus explained that those who come to him are drawn by the Father (John 6:44). Exactly how the Father does it may be a case-by-case matter. God knows each of us and can choose whatever works best for each of us to draw us to Jesus. Nonetheless, the most powerful draw that the Father uses to reach individuals, and ultimately, as Jesus said, all people, is the love expressed by giving his life for all on the cross.

-2-

Jesus' Love

Jesus Loves Me by Anna B. Warner and William B. Bradbury, published in 1862, is one of the most popular Christian hymns of all time around the world. The poetic declaration:

> Jesus loves me this I know
> For the Bible tells me so

appears in poems, books, and sermons by numerous authors.
The refrain:

> Yes, Jesus loves me,
> Yes, Jesus loves me,
> Yes, Jesus loves me,
> The Bible tells me so

is sung by many artists using various styles in different scenarios. The song is but one of many, including *Jesus Loves the Little Children*, *What a Friend We Have in Jesus*, and *Jesus is Love* that proclaim what many find to be a heartwarming message about Jesus Christ. In research, I found fewer instances of such sentiments about God the Father in the several lists I consulted of the most popular Christian hymns.

Jesus, it seems, warmly attracts people even when they feel negatively against churches or Christianity as a religion. In the novel, *The Lion the Witch and the Wardrobe*,[10] one of the *Chronicles of Narnia* by C. S. Lewis, three of the four children reacted warmly when they heard the name Aslan for the first time, without knowing this lion, Lewis' symbolic depiction of Jesus. The fourth child, temporarily influenced by the evil personality in the land, reacted negatively. Lewis allegorized, through these children, different human reactions to Jesus Christ. I recall the different feelings I experienced about Jesus during my

---

[10] C. S. Lewis, *The Lion, the Witch and the Wardrobe*, Great Brittain, 1950.

childhood. When as a preschooler my older sister mentioned him, I was curious. Ten years later as a teen, when the negative experience of church was still fresh in my mind, I did not want to hear about Jesus. Afterward, when I was moved to seriously inquire about the relevancy of God, I felt warmed to Jesus, especially on Christmas Eve as I thought about him, the infant gift from God to save the world.

The New Testament propagates the message of Jesus' love in nearly all of its books. The Gospels of Matthew, Mark, and Luke emphasize Jesus' compassion for the sick people he healed and the hungry people he fed. The Gospel of John mentions Jesus' love for those close to him and the special things he did to express it. All of the Gospel accounts of Jesus' death on the cross remind readers of his love for humanity for which he gave himself as a sacrifice, and all contain his teachings about loving other people. The same is true of the Epistles of Paul, Peter, and especially John. Time and space here does not allow a complete examination of the many passages, but we will examine a few that make the point.

Nearly one fifth of John's Gospel is spent on the last night that Jesus spent with his disciples before his arrest. Together, they shared a meal, participated in a long discussion, and traveled to the Garden of Gethsemane. Early that evening, Jesus surprised his disciples by rising from the table, changing his outerwear to that of a servant, and proceeding to wash his disciples' feet. Only John records this event that we can read about in the 13th Chapter. Most readers who are familiar with John's Gospel recognize this occasion as what is called "the foot washing." Indeed, Jesus washed twenty four dusty, smelly, feet that evening, but only when we consider what John wrote immediately before and after the event can we grasp the significance. Before it John wrote:

> It was just before the Passover Festival. Jesus knew that the hour had come for him to leave this world and go to the Father. Having loved his own who were in the world, he loved them to the end.

Jesus' love is the backdrop of this unusual event. Through his unexpected, somewhat upsetting act, he brought it out and put it on display. It is one thing to say, I love you, and in words the expression is beautiful, but demonstrating love portrays it more potently. In Western culture, when a man loves a woman and wants to make her his lifetime bride, he proposes, kneeling on one knee before the delighted woman, extending his hand toward her, affectionately gazing, uttering these never-to-be-forgotten words after softly saying her name—"I love you; will you marry me?" His romantic actions augment his words.

The comparison is not exact, but Jesus, wearing the garments of a servant, kneeling before his disciples, washing their feet, potently expressed his love for them. Indeed, he was willing to humble himself for them and serve them, but I think there was more to it than even these benevolent expressions. The washing of their feet was a symbolic act of his entire life, starting with his self-abasing, self-sacrificing divestment of glory that eternally he enjoyed as the Son of God with the Father; continuing with his Incarnation—entering human existence as an unborn baby in his mother, Mary's womb; proceeding with birth and childhood in all the weakness and vulnerabilities that accompany them; on to adulthood, experiencing along the way all of the troubles that a full human life encounters, including the death of his step father, Joseph; and, in grand conclusion, on the verge of the ultimate expression of self-sacrifice, his imminent death on the cross. Paul captured it all in Philippians 2:5-8:

> … Christ Jesus: Who, being in very nature God, did not consider equality with God something to be used to his own advantage; rather, he made himself nothing by taking the very nature of a servant, being made in human likeness. And being found in appearance as a man, he humbled himself by becoming obedient to death—even death on a cross!

Nothing in human experience compares. To have expressed love in this way, Jesus had to start with the glory that was innate to his divinity and deliberately lay it—the glory—aside. This was the start of what Jesus called "laying down his life" (John 10:15). Taking on fragile, weak, mortal, creaturely humanity was an unimaginable degradation, but Jesus took it to an even deeper level by diving to the depth of human servant-hood. Even then he was not finished until he went on to the ultimate expression—completely laying down his life for those he loved. Though the Father sent him to do it, he actually accomplished it voluntarily—he didn't have to do it (John 10:18).

It's no wonder that songs were written about his love!

Having washed the feet of his amazed and confused disciples, Jesus restored his attire, resumed his place at the table, and proceeded to explain his actions. For years, along with others, I practiced foot-washing as an annual reminder of the lesson of humility that Jesus taught his disciples. Year after year, we emphasized serving as we washed each other's feet. Service is an important and needed virtue, but when Jesus began to elaborate on his act that evening, he had more in mind. He had modeled for his disciples his life of love-motivated servant-hood, giving them an example that he wanted them to follow. Was Jesus' point that his disciples should behave like good servants? Reading the discussion that ensued about Judas' impending act of betrayal can mask the main point, which John records in v. 34, "A new command I give you: Love one another. As I have loved you, so you must love one another." If, when reading the 13th Chapter from the beginning, we do not see the connection between the foot-washing and the mandate to love, we miss the point. Jesus' life was all about love, which he expressed by self-sacrifice. When he washed the disciples' feet, demonstrating the fullness of his self-sacrificing love for them, he demonstrated that they were to follow him in this life of self-sacrifice. How? By loving each other as Jesus had loved them.

The long conversation that night, recorded by John in the four chapters that followed, returned to this theme of self-sacrificing love several more times. First, when Jesus foretold the coming of the Holy Spirit to be with the disciples as "another Counselor," he repeated three times his injunction that they obey his command to love (14:15, 21, 23-24). A little later, as Jesus used a vine with its branches to explain to his disciples the relationship between himself and them, he reiterated this injunction, emphasizing the self-sacrificial nature of this love (15:10, 12-13). Finally, in Jesus' prayer, which the next Chapter explores in detail, he prayed about the manifestation of that love in his disciples and all those throughout history who would follow him.

The Father's Love

The Christian hymns mentioned above extol Jesus' love for Christians, and indeed they should, but it may come as a surprise to some that the New Testament tells about Jesus extolling the Father's love for him and revealing amazing truths about the Father's love for humanity.

Matthew, Mark, and Luke consistently tell the story of a voice from heaven uttering, "my Son, whom I love" at Jesus' baptism (Matthew 3:17; Mark 1:11; Luke 3:22). A similar utterance, recorded by the same Gospel writers, occurred at Jesus' transfiguration—the temporary brightening of his appearance in divine glory (Matthew 17:5; Mark 9:7; Luke 9:35). In human history, no such heavenly utterance about God's love for a human had been reported. In recording these unique events, the Gospel writers proclaimed declarations from heaven about the human Jesus, declarations hinting to the misinformed human race that in spite of beliefs about the angry disposition of deity toward humanity, the astounding truth was about to be revealed.

Jesus himself was the revealer, sent specifically to make known the truth about God, his Father. Matthew 11:27 quotes Jesus, saying, "No one knows the Son except the Father, and no one knows the Father except the Son and those to whom the Son chooses to reveal him." Remarkable statement! Jesus told Peter that his realization of Jesus' identity as "the Christ, the Son of the living God" (Matthew 16:17) was through the revelation from the Father. Otherwise, Jesus' identity was not humanly discernable. Jesus further asserted that in spite of the revelations given to Abraham, Isaac, Jacob, Moses, and all of the prophets, only Jesus knows the Father. Who, then, did these men of God know as El Shaddai, I AM, Elohim, Adonai, and Yahweh? They knew whatever had been revealed to them, but none of them considered the God they knew as either **Father** or **Son** of God. It took the Father to reveal the Son in his true identity, and in the same way, it took the Son to reveal the Father.

In the Sermon on the Mount, recorded in Matthew 5 through 7, Jesus taught his followers about God, repeatedly referring to him by the title "Father," again and again preceding "Father" with possessive pronouns that directly associated the humans in his audience with this Father. For example, the Lord's Prayer starts with "Our Father in heaven" (Matthew 6:9). Jesus talked about a Father in relationship with his children, one who is deeply interested in those who genuinely trust him, one who blesses, answers prayer, and is absolutely trustworthy. The message that Matthew recorded from Jesus was full of surprises and amazing revelations about God, concluding in 7:28-29 with, "When Jesus had finished saying these things, the crowds were amazed at his teaching, because he taught as one who had authority, and not as their teachers of the law." These teachers read about Israel's God in the Hebrew Scriptures and taught what they understood, but Jesus, Son of God, sharing divinity with the Father and the Holy Spirit, possessed first-hand insight into all of the things that pertain to being Israel's God. That is one reason why he spoke with such authority.

Consider this simple illustration: When I was a pre-teen, I played on a Little League baseball team that my dad coached. Kids loved my dad. He diligently worked with them in practice, making them better players. Year after year his teams enjoyed the reputation of being among the best. As his son, I witnessed first hand my dad's genuine love for all of the kids that he coached. Teaching children, including his own, was his passion. Johnny, one of my closest friends in school, loved baseball and desperately wanted to play on my dad's team. He liked me, but I think his strongest motivation for friendship with me was that I was the coach's son. Persistently, he bombarded me with questions about my dad, and I would try my best to answer, only to trigger more curious questions. He could watch our team as we played, and observe my dad as he coached, but Johnny could not possibly know my dad as I did. This illustration of my relationship with my dad falls far short of Jesus' relationship with the Father, but I use it here to emphasize the point that Jesus' revelations about the Father were substantially more insightful than everything that the people had learned from their teachers. The Son of God came from heaven to tell humanity what God was really like.

Two thousand years ago much of the world was under Roman rule and dominated by Greek culture. Religion, regardless of the gods worshipped, was about acquiring the blessing and protection of the gods.[11] The Greek god of the sky and father of gods was Zeus, and the Roman equivalent was Jupiter. Throughout history, artists and sculptors depicted this father god as an old man with a long white beard and usually holding a lightning bolt like a spear about to be thrown down from the sky. The Jewish people generally rejected the gods of the Greco-Roman world in favor of the God of Israel, mentioned by Paul to Greek worshippers as, "The God who made the world and everything in it... the Lord of heaven and earth" (Acts 17:24). Paul used common Greek words for deity – *Theos* for God and *Kyrios* for Lord as pronounced in English. Jewish scholars and teachers deliberately avoided attempts to pronounce the sacred names written in the Hebrew Scriptures. When Jesus spoke of "your Father" in the Sermon on

---

[11] James S. Jeffers, *The Greco-Roman World of the New Testament Era* (Downers Grove, IL: InterVarsity Press, 1999), 90. "Ancient religion began as a religion of farmers. It grew out of sacrifices and ceremonies invented to bless the fields. The ancients believed that they were surrounded and protected, or threatened, by many invisible powers. Their ceremonies either called upon the gods for help or kept them at bay."

the Mount, he used the same word that his listeners used for a human father in everyday conversation. Although the Jews had a concept of the fatherhood of God toward those who fear him, Jesus' use of "Father" in such a personal way went way beyond that concept. In the Sermon on the Mount, Jesus spoke of God as one who carried on a relationship with human beings in ways that were uncommon in rabbinical teaching.

When Jesus spoke of the special relationship that he enjoyed with God the Father, his statements were even stronger. The Gospel of John quotes many such statements that Jesus made to his audiences in Jerusalem, particularly those who questioned, criticized, or condemned his assertions. To these listeners, Jesus boldly declared the love that the Father has for him: "The Father loves the Son and has placed everything in his hands" (3:35). Again, "For the Father loves the Son and shows him all he does" (5:20). His audience did not receive these statements as if they were common expressions of a Rabbi. John wrote, "For this reason the Jews tried all the harder to kill him; not only was he breaking the Sabbath, but he was even calling God his own Father, making himself equal with God" (5:18). Those who opposed him in Jerusalem considered such statements as blasphemous. To them Jesus said, "I have come in my Father's name, and you do not accept me" (5:43). John records highly contentious conversations that went on over the months preceding Jesus' final visit to Jerusalem to be crucified. One day in a temple court, a Pharisee railed, "Where is your father?" to which Jesus replied, "You do not know me or my Father" (8:19). Jesus made clear to this religious leader and those backing him that he was not referring to their concept of the fatherhood of God. As the conversation continued, and Jesus spoke of the one who sent him as if that someone was intimately close to him, they were confused: "They did not understand that he was telling them about the Father" (8:27).

These religious leaders were struggling because the conversation was so unusual. It was as if the two parties were speaking in different languages. Jesus understood them, but they did not understand him. His perspective was other-worldly as he spoke about an intimate relationship with one who they envisioned as transcendent. Furthermore, Jesus' statements such as the following came across as insulting: "My Father, whom you claim as your God" (8:54), and "Though you do not know him, I know him" (8:55). Jesus simply told the truth, but to these religious bigots, the truth insulted them and ran counter to their viewpoint of God. Their anger grew so intense that they were about to stone him before Jesus left the scene.

John summarized Jesus' time on earth in 1:10-11:

> He was in the world, and though the world was made through him, the world did not recognize him. He came to that which was his own, but his own did not receive him.

The created did not recognize the Creator; the covenant people did not receive the Lord of the Covenant. The world has not yet gotten over this close encounter with the heavenly kind. Therein lays the explanation of the reality that is so difficult for us to get: God **loves** us! The Son of God visited to announce it to us, openly declaring that this love was something that he knew and experienced constantly, revealing that this same love prodigiously applies to humanity, but religion simply couldn't handle this astounding truth.

Consequently, Jesus concentrated on ensuring that his followers knew and experienced this truth. Shortly before his arrest, he said to them, "I am not alone, for my Father is with me" (John 16:32). In the long conversation earlier that evening, Jesus reminded his followers of the Father's love for him. Just before he uttered these words about the Father being with him, he assured his followers, "the Father himself loves you because you have loved me" (16:27). In the next chapter, as we investigate Jesus' prayer, we will see the amazing way that Jesus described this love and his intent that it is experienced by those who follow

Jesus today. For now, we must address the question: Is God's love only for those who love Jesus?

Consider again the pagan father of the gods in Greco-Roman religion, whose hand holds, as artistically depicted, a lightning bolt, an instrument of terror or destruction. Those who worshipped this god did not imagine him as a loving father. Even the fatherhood of God concept in worshippers of the God of Israel did not foster a perception anything like the Father that Jesus revealed. Contrast these human perceptions with Jesus' words in John 3:16: "God so loved the world that he gave his one and only Son, that whoever believes in him shall not perish but have eternal life." With these words, Jesus unleashed a new concept about the scope of God's love for the whole of humanity, not just a limited group. This God is willing to do whatever it takes for all humans, as many as are willing to accept his gift, to be rescued from the inevitable death that we all face, replacing it with life forever, life unlike anything presently known in this time and place, life with the very Creator in Paradise, life experienced at the grand conclusion of transformation into the likeness of Jesus, perfect in character, full of love, joy, and peace, life shared in reunion with precious loved ones and friends. The offer seems too good to be true, the sacrifice too great to comprehend!

As a father, it is unfathomable to me that I would give my daughter or son for someone else! The idea defies nature itself. Many animals express affection, care, protection, and devotion to their offspring. Some animals defend their offspring at the expense of their own lives. Who among us would give any of our beloved children for someone else?

John 3:16 is quoted so often that it is easy to overlook its significance. Does God really love humans that much? If our parents or grandparents tell us that they love us, difficult as it is for parents to constantly express love regardless of circumstances, even toward their children that they cherish, we usually believe them. Nonetheless strangely, we have a problem believing God. Yet, we are assured in the Bible that he does not lie (Hebrews

6:18), he is impartial (Acts 10:34), and even if our human parents fail us, God never will (Psalm 27:10).

The passage says, "God **so** loved the world." Just how much is **so**? The utterly incomprehensible answer: "that he gave his one and only Son" for it. How difficult was that for God?

The story of Jesus by the New Testament writers is written from a down-here perspective. What was it like up-there? What was it like when King Herod decided to take the life of baby Jesus, and the angel was sent to warn Joseph to take the child to Egypt (Matthew 2:13-14)? What was that journey like? How difficult was the stay in Egypt? I suppose we could assume that it was easy for God, but was it? The Psalmist wrote, "As a father has compassion on his children, so the LORD has compassion on those who fear him" (Psalm 103:13). Jesus' Father does not worry or feel the effect of emotion as we, but in his own way he surely felt for his infant Son. What was it like from heaven's perspective for young Jesus to be mistakenly left behind in Jerusalem when he was only 12 years old (Luke 2:41-49)? How did heaven react when Jesus cried out in the Garden of Gethsemane, "Father, if you are willing, take this cup from me; yet not my will, but yours be done" (Luke 22:42)? Luke continues the narrative of this painful prayerful exchange:

> "An angel from heaven appeared to him and strengthened him. And being in anguish, he prayed more earnestly, and his sweat was like drops of blood falling to the ground" (22:43-44).

I could go on with the torture and crucifixion. As Jesus prayed on the cross, what was it like in heaven? I will leave it to the reader to imagine.

These scenes represent only a few snapshots of Jesus' life on earth and the intertwined involvement of heaven as he faced hazards, pain, and untold difficulties. The Father's gift of his one and only Son was immeasurably costly and inconceivably difficult. The love that motivated this gift is indescribable.

Indeed, God is Love

This chapter's title is *Jesus' Love*. Although the first part was specifically about Jesus Christ and his marvelous way of expressing love, the larger part of this chapter is about the love of the less-visible Person of the one triune God—the Father. The number of words or space allocated for these two parts are no indication of the quality or extent of love. As John put it in his first epistle, "God is love" (1 John 4:16). God is Father, Son, and Spirit. The love of God itself is one and is expressed as such through the distinct Persons of the Trinity. There is no three-part separation, quantification, or distinction of that love. We have seen the Bible's statements about the love of Jesus and the love of the Father. Although far little is written about the Holy Spirit, it is not difficult to ascertain the Spirit's love. For example, John quoted in 14:16-17 what Jesus said about the Spirit:

> I will ask the Father, and he will give you another advocate to help you and be with you forever— the Spirit of truth. The world cannot accept him, because it neither sees him nor knows him. But you know him, for he lives with you and will be in you.

In saying "another" advocate, Jesus implied that there was a previous advocate. He was speaking of himself. He is the Advocate or Counselor—similar to the role of a lawyer—who serves as a helper for human sinners (1 John 2:1). Because he was about to leave earth to return to heaven, he reassured his disciples that the Spirit of Truth, would come along side and be with the disciples as Jesus had been. And Jesus promised that the Spirit would be with them forever. Because of his invisibility, only the follower of Jesus would perceive the presence of the Holy Spirit; he would be incognito to the world. But to the follower of Jesus, in whom the Holy Spirit dwells, Paul wrote, "do not grieve the Holy Spirit of God" (Ephesians 4:30). How can one grieve the Holy Spirit? Paul's admonishment at the beginning of Ephesians 4 had to do with preserving the oneness of the Spirit, by whom the Church is one body. The remainder of this chapter details what it looks like to preserve this oneness, without which the Holy Spirit can be grieved. As in all cases, these words have not been perfectly kept in the Church, so if the Holy Spirit remains forever in the Church even when grieved, that is evidence of the grace and love of God the Spirit seen also in the Father and Jesus.

Truly, God is love, and it is good for us to recognize that love in all three Persons of the Trinity.

Nonetheless, I believe that it is appropriate to conclude this chapter with a revived discussion about Jesus and his love. Of the Persons of the Trinity, only Jesus is human, only he lived a human life on earth, and only he is one of us. For that reason, we relate to him in a way that we could not relate to the Father and Spirit. Before creation, this was the design and purpose of God, as Paul explained in Colossians 1:15-20:

> The Son is the image of the invisible God, the firstborn over all creation. For in him all things were created: things in heaven and on earth, visible and invisible, whether thrones or powers or rulers or authorities; all things have been created through him and for him. He is before all things, and in him all things hold together. And he is the head of the body, the church; he is the beginning and the firstborn from among the dead, so that in everything he might have the supremacy. For God was pleased to have all his fullness dwell in him, and through him to reconcile to himself all things, whether things on earth or things in heaven, by making peace through his blood, shed on the cross.

As Paul wrote, God is invisible to our eyes, but humans were able to see the Son of God because Jesus is human. He preceded creation, creating everything that has been created. This Person of the Trinity was and is the out-front one toward the created order, and the Trinity agreed it to be so. Understandably, we, who have blood, relate to blood and what it means for it to be shed. We even understand that the blood of one shed for another is extraordinary, because it is part of both religious rites and war. We honor soldiers whose lives were sacrificed for us on the battlefield. Because all of the fullness of God is in Jesus, it is perfectly good and appropriate for us to recognize first in him God's love by what he demonstrated to us.

It is this love that gives us every reason to pay attention to his prayer for those he loved.

Jesus' Prayer

Twelve years ago, I wrote the following letter to my then three-year old grandson, Jason.

September 8, 2004

Dear Jason:

At the age of three, you began to appreciate opportunities to hang out with me. By the time you read this letter, you may not relate to the phrase, "hang out," but it is a colloquial expression for being around.

Maybe it is because I often get down on the floor and play with you as much as I can at your level. I think that might be a consequence of me being one of 17 children of my parents and the fifth at that. I had a lot of younger brothers and sisters and got used to playing with them.

Recently, you have shown such an interest in being with me that you are willing to leave play with Grandma or Janeen and even a video program to join me in my bedroom when I am on my knees in prayer.

I can hear your footsteps as you come down the hall, often running. You open the door without asking and come in. You are not deterred by my activity, which it seems to me would bore most three year olds. No, you come over and kneel down beside me. Often, I invite you to do so, and you are always willing.

I stop whatever I am saying to God, and begin to thank Him for you. I pick you up in my arms and hold you as I continue to pray for you. I enjoy this because I think God does. I am deeply touched by your desire to be in God's company along with Grandpa.

You are not the first child that has joined me in prayer, but you are the only one who likes to do it.

At times, picking up on things that I say, you repeat them with strong passion. You even prostrate yourself on the floor as you continue to call out to "Father" and "Jesus" or "Lord" for help.

After a while, you get tired and climb up on the bed. There you will lie for a while and let me go on praying. You still are not bored. You don't ask me to get up and leave the room with you to play, as you often do when I am working in my office. You seem to fully understand that this time is special.

Thanks for joining and helping me in prayer,

Grandpa

This is one of 42 letters from *Dear Jason*,[12] a book that I wrote and published the first edition in 2010. I use it here to introduce the topic of Jesus' prayer. Not that I consider myself one to compare with Jesus, but the relationship between Jason and his grandpa, as illustrated in this letter, is somewhat allegorical of the relationship of humanity to Jesus.

A loving relationship surrounds Jason's time with me in prayer. He likes to be with me because he knows that I love him. I enjoy his presence with me because I sense his love and, as his grandpa, I love him "to bits;" he is "the apple of my eye;" I cherish him. When he entered the room and knelt at my side, I wanted to pick him up, hold him in my arms, and lift him toward heaven as I prayed for him. My love for him does not equal Jesus' love for his disciples, but I can imagine similar sentiments. Figuratively, in Jesus' prayer, he lifted up his beloved and held them high before the Father. He did this nearly 2000 years ago for those with him then, and he has done the same for everyone who has followed him since, including today in the 21st Century.

As explained in the previous chapter, Jesus is love, and he revealed to humanity the Father—God in an intimate relationship with human beings whom he loves. Five chapters in John's Gospel, Chapters 13-17, jam-packed with details of the long discussion between Jesus and his disciples on the night of his betrayal, display love as both the backdrop and the foreground of the conversations. Chapter 17, Jesus' prayer, concludes this discussion. Let's take a deep look at this prayer, starting with the events that led up to it.[13]

---

[12] Martin S. Manuel, *Dear Jason* (2013), Kindle edition location 1536, available at Amazon.com

[13] Biblical quotations in this chapter are from the New American Standard Bible (NASB), New International Version (NIV), and New Revised Standard Version (NRSV). These translations have subtle differences in wording that I found relevant to the explanations and conclusions that follow.

Background and Context of John 17

From the time of Jesus' baptism, and through the next several years, he ministered to all who came to him, mostly in Galilee—the province north of Judea, occasionally traveling to Jerusalem for short visits there, especially around the time of the Jewish festivals. John records in Chapter 7 Jesus' trip to attend the Feast of Tabernacles in Jerusalem during the last year of his earthly ministry. The religious authorities in Jerusalem had been looking for an opportunity to put him to death; nonetheless, although Jesus was aware of their intentions, after the festival, he fearlessly remained in Jerusalem through the winter, tirelessly teaching the crowds in the temple courts, enduring the persistent attacks of his critics, patiently sharing with them the truth of his identity that again and again they rejected (John 7-10). As spring approached, Jesus left for a short stay east of Jerusalem, putting space between himself and those men intent upon killing him, planning to return to Jerusalem for the Passover. Meanwhile, the priests and Sanhedrin—the council of religious leaders—expecting him to show up for the spring festival, having become intolerant of his popularity and intimidated by his personal power, developed sinister plans to get rid of Jesus (John 11:47-53).

Shortly before the Passover, Jesus returned, descending from the Mount of Olives in symbolic triumph. The reaction there was strong. John wrote in Chapter 12 about a large crowd of Jews gathering after hearing that Jesus was on the way, deserting the religious leadership in Jerusalem and, instead, leaping upon the Jesus-of-Nazareth bandwagon. They lined up along the road he was traveling, riding on the back of a young donkey, fulfilling an ancient Messianic prophecy. The procession of his followers grew as the crowd swelled. Cheers, chants, songs erupted into a loud celebration. To their dismay, the Pharisees said, "the whole world has gone after him" (John 12:19). Jerusalem was near an uproar. Even some Greek worshippers there took note of Jesus. With this crescendo of events, Jesus remarked, "The hour has come for the Son of Man to be glorified... But I, when I am lifted up from the earth, will draw all men to myself" (John 12:23, 32).

He clearly saw that the time had come for his prophesied crucifixion in Jerusalem, but he realized the victory he would achieve through death.

A few days later, as Jesus dined with his 12 disciples, engaging them in a lengthy farewell discussion recorded in chapters 13-16, he startled them with powerful symbolic actions and shocking statements. During this special supper, as described in Chapter 2 of this book, Jesus lovingly washed the disciples' feet, symbolically depicting the entirety of his love-motivated, self-sacrificing life; he sadly foretold his impending betrayal, sparking in his disciples an emotional reaction that continued through the evening; and he firmly commanded the disciples to love each other as he loves them, the fulfillment of the foot-washing symbolism (John 13:3-34). The disciples, distressed at the realization of Jesus' imminent departure, seeming to overlook the lesson Jesus was trying to teach, pressed him for details about the trouble ahead and its effect on Jesus (John 13:36). Jesus encouraged them, promising a joyful reunion, sharing amazing insights of His intimate relationship with God the Father, and showing the stunning intent of the triune God to unite with them through the Holy Spirit (John 14:1-27). Jesus knew that the disciples would not comprehend much of these stupendous revelations then, but that later it all would sink in and they would understand (John 13:7, 36; 14:11, 20, 26).

Leaving the meeting place, they started walking toward the olive grove, the garden of Gethsemane, where they frequently met. Along the way, Jesus continued the discussion, using the analogy of a vine to explain His relationship with them and their need to remain in it (John 15:1-8). The stunning analogy must have imprinted an unforgettable image on the minds of the disciples, as they realized their union with Jesus and complete dependency on him even after his departure. In that context, he repeated and reemphasized his command that they love each other as he loves them (John 15:9-17). Then he warned them that they would not be accepted by the world (John 15:18-16:4), but, reminding them of what previously he had told them about the impending gift of the Holy Spirit after His glorification, he gave them a few more details (John 15:26; 16:5-15). Finally, he wrapped up the conversation with encouraging words about the events of the upcoming days, events that cast a mood of gloom over the disciples, but Jesus assured them that the outcome would lift them to new joy (John 16:16-33).

Overview of Jesus' Prayer

At that point in this astonishing discussion on that most poignant night, Jesus turned His eyes and attention from His disciples to His Father in heaven.   In the presence of these disciples, Jesus looked up and started to speak, uttering from His mouth words that expressed profound reverence, respect, and adoration.   The first word, "Father," underscored the whole experience of the Son of God's existence in eternity.   That existence "with God" while being God—the Logos or Word—was expressed in Jesus' human life and witnessed by John and the other disciples. John wrote, "We have seen his glory, the glory of the Only Begotten [NIV84 margin], who came from the Father, full of grace and truth" (John 1:14). John personally saw in Jesus the glory of God. It was not in a radiant face as described in the first chapter of the book of Revelation, but in what Jesus displayed outwardly of His inner self—signs his disciples recognized as evidence of God's glory within him (John 2:11).

This Jesus is the human who uttered, "Father, the time has come."   The time?   The time for His return to the Father he adored. To grasp the thought is breathtaking! Robert H. Mounce wrote: "Chapter 17, perhaps more than any other section of John, reveals the strong bonds of unity and mutual love between the Father and Son."[14]   The underlying foundation of this prayer is found in v. 1, where Jesus referred to "the only true God" (John 17:3) as "Father."   He did the same in vv. 5, 11, 20, 24, and 25. Additionally, he used the second person pronoun and second

---

[14] Robert H. Mounce, *The Expositor's Bible Commentary Revised Edition* "John" (Grand Rapids, MI: Zondervan, 2006), volume 10, 597.

person possessive pronoun a total of 48 times. It is entirely about relationship between the Father and him—before His earthly ministry, during it, and forever. The opening words of this prayer unveil the extent of this relationship.

Scholars say this prayer is organized into three parts: Jesus' prayer for himself (1-5), for his disciples (6-19), and for those who will come to believe (20-26).[15] However, not all agree on exactly which verses are in the first and second parts. Francis J. Moloney mentions a slightly different arrangement: verses 1-8, 9-19, 20-26.[16] Either view is acceptable to me. Instead of choosing one over the other, I chose in this book to focus on the third part, which both views mentioned consider 20-26.[17] Regarding 1-5, I consider the "prayer for himself" more fittingly considered a prayer about the oneness he and the Father enjoy that was about to become even more intimate.

First part: Jesus loved the Father, speaking to Him reverent words, resonating with deep respect, spoken in underlying devotedly loyal tones, desiring mutual glorification, longing for the return to the glory with the Father enjoyed together for all eternity. The conversation was like a telephone call between two intimate lovers, one saying, "I'm coming home and am excitedly looking forward to seeing you," the one on the other end saying, "Yes and I can hardly wait!" That's the kind of thing that was going on here—Jesus' great anticipation to return to be with the Father (John 17:1-5).

Along with this underlying tone of love are honest statements about the fulfillment of the mission. Supervisors in large American corporations often conclude projects or periods of work with performance evaluations. In such cases, usually the supervisor gives the employee an assessment of the work, whether it was completed on time and with the expected quality.

---

[15] Mounce, 597.

[16] Frances J. Moloney, *Love in the Gospel of John* (Grand Rapids, MI: Baker Academic, 2013). , Kindle location 2329.

[17] I will analyze only 20-23, considering 24-26 a conclusion of the prayer.

This scene was different; Jesus reported to the Father that the mission had been accomplished (John 17:4).

Second part: At the same time, Jesus reported to the Father that the disciples had met the Father's intentions. They had received and obeyed the words from the Father through Jesus. They had realized that the Father gave Jesus everything and that Jesus came from, and was sent by, the Father (John 17:6-8). Thus, they were ready for Jesus' departure and the next stage of their mission.

Several years before this evening, Jesus carefully had chosen his disciples. With him at the time were the Twelve minus Judas (John 13:29-31). They had spent the most profound evening together, Jesus pouring his love upon them (John 13:1). This part of the prayer was specifically for them. He had come from eternity in heaven to save the world, loved by the Father, but this part of the prayer was not for the world. Out of the world, the Father had chosen these individuals and given them to Jesus for the great mission. Jesus' prayer at this point was focused on them. He was departing, but they would remain. They would need God to sustain them.

N. T. Wright wrote that a loving mother, temporarily leaving her children with their grandparents, explains each child and how to care for them, not because she doesn't trust the grandparents but because she does. So, Jesus entrusted his disciples to his trustworthy and faithful Father.[18] But Jesus did not limit this request for them to protection, nor was he asking the Father simply to keep them together as a flock of sheep. He asked that they would be **one** as the Father and Jesus (John 17:9-11), a lot more than simply taking care of them. Jesus had asked for the humanly impossible. Had humans ever in history retained a bond of unity in love? In God's dealings with the Patriarchs and Prophets, he chose one person and worked everything through him or her. These individuals had others to assist them, but they were given hierarchical authority over the other humans.

---

[18] Tom Wright, *John for Everyone, Part 2: Chapters 11-21* (Great Brittain: Society for the Promotion of Christian Knowledge, 2002), 94-95.

Oneness was not essential to their missions. Jesus was working in a whole new way—with a group or team of people—where no hierarchy existed among these apostles.[19] This group, twelve at first, but a steadily growing number of followers in addition to the apostles, needed to function as one.

Again, Jesus reported that he had protected them while he was with them—the exception being Judas, as Scripture had foretold (John 17:12). Jesus asked the Father to set His followers apart from the world by the truth (John 17:13-19). N. T. Wright again helps our understanding of this request by explaining that as Jesus was set apart—consecrated like the Jewish High Priest—he requested that these disciples similarly be set apart by the Father. His disciples were to be holy and set apart for God's service. They were not part of the God-rejecting world.[20]

At this point, Jesus looked ahead, beyond the days, months, and years of the apostles ministries, way ahead—as we have come to realize—dozens and hundreds of years, and prayed for those believers who would come later through the ministry of the apostles, those who would become known as the Church. We will now analyze the four verses specific to this group of people.

John 17:20-23

> NRSV: I ask not only on behalf of these, but also on behalf of those who will believe in me through their word, that they may all be one. As you, Father, are in me and I am in you, may they also be in us, so that the world may believe that you have sent me. The glory that you have given me I have given them, so that they may be one, as we are one, I in them and you in me, that they may become completely one, so that the world may

---

[19] Galatians 2:8 mentions God's work in Peter as leader among equals. Paul, James, and John also had special leadership roles, but the Church did not have an individual leader as much as it had a team of leaders.

[20] Tom Wright, 96.

know that you have sent me and have loved them
even as you have loved me.

Third part: Jesus specifically expressed his love for the
Church through all time, followers of Jesus who would come
through the ministry of the apostles and their pastoral descendants
after Jesus' ascension.

**<u>Verse 20</u>: "I ask not only on
behalf of these, but also on
behalf of those who will believe
in me through their word,"**

"I ask not only on behalf of these, but also on behalf of":
Although the eleven apostles were with Jesus, and the second part
of his prayer was specifically for them, he went on to include
those who would come afterward, those in Jerusalem in the early
days of the Church, those in areas surrounding Jerusalem as the
Gospel spread, those throughout the Roman Empire and
beyond—the multiple thousands as the first Century closed, and
those in the many centuries since—multiple millions throughout
the world.

"Those who will believe in me": The Greek word *pisteuo*
translated "believe" in John's Gospel, and most of the New
Testament, is the verb form of the Greek word *pistis*, a noun
translated "faith" throughout the New Testament. The two words
share a common base like two sides of the same coin. Belief is
often thought of as mental acceptance of an idea, but these Greek
words have to do with a matter much stronger than mental
acceptance: *pisteuo* and *pistis* are about trust. To John and the
New Testament writers, believing is exercising trust in Jesus as
the Son of God sent as a human for human salvation.

Witness a hungry infant's excitement as she is drawn toward
her mother's breast for nursing, and you will see explicit trust in
action. The infant anticipates the warm, sweet taste of her
mother's milk to satisfy the discomfort of thirst and hunger she

feels. To the nursing baby, only mother offers this urgent and utmost need; a thumb may feel comforting, but it cannot feed; at that age, everything is simple. Without saying a word the child expresses complete trust in mommy to supply her need. Perhaps that is one reason that Jesus said, "the kingdom of God belongs to such as these" (Mark 10:14). To trust is to be confident in one who is trustworthy—one who delivers on commitments, who keeps promises, who fulfills responsibilities. To trust Jesus with their lives his followers must know enough about him to be certain of his abilities and sure that he does not need help—not from outside forces and not from themselves.

How encouraging it is to realize that this prayer was specifically for all those who trust in Jesus! His words here include 21st-century Christians, as well as all believers before and all who will follow. In fact, the Greek expression that John used translated "will believe" is a present participle verb, depicting these believers through all time, as if present, and indeed to Jesus, believers through all time were present before him as he was praying!

So much of what we read in the Gospels is Jesus speaking directly to His followers then and specifically to the Twelve. These words of Jesus in prayer are not for the Twelve or his followers then, but on behalf of his followers who were to come later. That includes committed Christians today! Jesus had all of his followers on his mind that night; his love for those who would later follow him was as strong as it was for those who shared that special evening with him. This may seem difficult to believe, but Jesus' words give assurance to all who have ever been or will be his followers.

"Through their word": The word, or message, of the apostles was the Gospel—the good news that Jesus Christ came for the salvation of all humanity. Jesus foresaw that his apostles would faithfully pass on this message, bringing about many believers. Previously, Jesus had predicted that believers would become "many seeds" through which "all" are drawn (John 12:24, 32). The apostles proclaimed the message first, reaching believers, who, in turn, proclaimed the message to others, who also became believers. Like seeds on the ground, spreading to fill a field, the message spread from person-to-person and from generation to the next generation. The implications are startling. Jesus was not speaking about a religion limited to certain parts of human society but, through the Gospel, a world changer that eventually envelopes the whole of humanity.

Verse 21: "that they may all be one. As you, Father, are in me and I am in you, may they also be in us, so that the world may believe that you have sent me."

"That they may all be one": His prayer was not that believers would join a church and strive to be a unified group. Nor was it about ecumenism or any other humanly-initiated effort toward oneness, including any personal effort. As Brown, Fitzmyer and Murphy explained, it is not "an expression of human solidarity or the creation of an institutional structure."[21] Instead, Jesus asked the **Father** to **give** oneness: otherwise, it would not have been stated in prayer. How can **all** be **one**? First and foremost, it is an act of God, with whom, all things are possible (Matthew 19:26).

Perhaps earlier that evening, Jesus described metaphorically to his disciples what he spoke straightforwardly in this prayer. He had said "I am the vine; you are the branches" (John 15:5). A vine is a single plant with many branches. The branches look unalike, vary in length and thickness, spread in different directions, but bear a common fruit. Branches are one with the vine. In this metaphor, Jesus beautifully depicted the relationship

---

[21] Raymond E. Brown, Joseph A. Fitzmyer, Roland E. Murphy, *The New Jerome Biblical Commentary* (Englewood Cliffs, NJ: Prentice-Hall, 1990), 979.

of each Church member to Jesus, the intimacy as well as the dependency.

Also, Jesus included the Father in this metaphor, calling him the gardener (15:1). Herein lays a clue of the Father's work to grant the oneness for which Jesus prayed. The gardener works directly with the branches to foster their health and stimulate their growth (15:2). As any good gardener lifts branches that droop, removes dead wood, and prunes the healthy—all so that the branches become more productive, the Father is directly involved with each Christian, granting conditions by which each grows to enjoy oneness through Jesus with all who share union in Christ—the Trinity and every member of the Church. Jesus reinforced the member's oneness with each other as John wrote in 15:9-12:

> As the Father has loved me, so I have loved you. Now remain in my love. If you obey my commands, you will remain in my love... My command is this: love each other as I have loved you.

The Father answers Jesus through his activity in the Church and in the individual lives of members. He lovingly cares for the whole Church and acts directly with members for their spiritual health, resulting in one fruitful vine full of healthy branches that through that vine share in one another.

"As you, Father, are in me and I am in you": Previously that evening, Jesus had told His disciples that he and the Father live in each other. The disciples did not understand, but Jesus offered as evidence the work that he had done (John 14:10-11). Jesus had revealed an amazing truth: the oneness of God in the diversity of Father and Son. Michael Jinkins explained this complex concept:

> In higher Trinitarian theology there is a word that describes the special kind of relationship among the persons of the Trinity: the Father, Son, and

Holy Spirit. The word is *perichoresis*. It is a Greek word that describes, literally, the interpenetration of each person of the Trinity in the other persons... These terms attempt to communicate a profound mystery of Christian theology: the mutual indwelling of the Father, Son, and Holy Spirit in one another.[22]

Jesus repeated this truth in prayer, but in the process revealed another amazing truth: that the relationship of indwelling between he and his Father—their oneness—would be shared.

"May they also be in us": This oneness now includes believers **in** the Father and **"in** Christ"—as other New Testament writers put it—**as** Jesus and the Father are in each other. About this request of humans indwelling God, Stephen Seamands wrote:

> Of course, the way God indwells human beings is qualitatively different from the way we indwell God. Miroslav Volf expresses the difference like this: 'The Spirit indwells human persons, whereas human beings by contrast indwell the life-giving ambiance of the Spirit, not the person of the Spirit.' Only God, he maintains, can truly indwell other persons.[23]

The vine analogy, explained above, that Jesus used earlier that evening, clarifies this truth: foreign to human and animal existence, the concept of one person living in another person might be more observable, at least in an allegorical way, in plant life. The concept is spiritual, thus no comparison in the physical

---

[22] Michael Jinkins, *Invitation to Theology* (Downers Grove, Il: InterVarsity Press, 2001), 91.

[23] Stephen Seamands, *Ministry in the Image of God* (Downers Grove, IL: InterVarsity Press, 2005), 145-146. Seamands' quote of Miraslav Volf is from *After Our Likeness,* (Grand Rapids, MI: Wm. B. Erdmans Publishing, 1998) 211.

realm is exact, but those who live it actually experience it, in a way, through their relationships.

"So that the world may believe that you have sent me": The effect of this oneness witnesses to the world (I will further pursue this in coming chapters). John mentioned the world frequently. The world was made through "the Word," who came into it, became human, and lived unrecognized among the rest of humans (John 1:10, 14). The world, consisting of unbelieving humans, hated Jesus and his disciples (John 15:18-19). Earlier in the prayer, Jesus plainly said that he was not praying for the world but for His disciples (John 17:9). But here, he shows that his intent is that the world believes in him through these disciples. In love, the Father had sent Jesus to save the world (John 3:17). Jesus here imparts insight of how his mission to save the world will extend, person by person, to everyone. It has yet to be finished, but we should neither mistake nor underestimate the intent. Furthermore, we must take note carefully of **how** Jesus prescribed this fulfillment: oneness of the disciples in the Father and Son.

Let us consider the depth of insight in these words of the Lord. Throughout human history, philosophy and religion have influenced culture. A global 2012 poll reported that 59% of the world's population is religious.[24] Neither religion nor philosophy has managed to enable humans to rise above the intrinsic characteristics of our nature so that unity and harmony would prevail in any society or group. If such an unnatural expression of human relationships actually occurred, the religion or philosophy that espoused it would stand out above all others; it would have a valid claim of being of divine origin. Jesus asked in prayer to His Father that His followers would have such a claim, and that the world would be the witness. Seamands explains: "As Christians, because of the oneness we have with the Father, Son, and Holy Spirit, we also experience spiritual unity with other believers beyond our general human capacity for oneness."[25]

---

[24] Wikipedia, "Religion" (August 2014). http://en.wikipedia.org/wiki/Religion .

[25] Seamands, 150.

How can this be seen in the Church and portrayed to the world? Seamands answers: "Koinonia, the Greek word for fellowship that John and other New Testament writers often use… implies an intensely close relationship with one another beyond mere human camaraderie."[26] Because humans are the lamps that display this oneness, it is not possible, humanly, to duplicate the perfect oneness of the Trinity. But light shining from a lamp—even an imperfect lamp—still unmistakably illuminates a dark place. The Jamieson, Fausset, and Brown Commentary puts it this way:

> But the Spirit of Christ, illuminating, transforming, and reigning in the hearts of the genuine disciples of Christ, drawing them to each other as members of one family, and prompting them to loving co-operation for the good of the world—this is what, when sufficiently glowing and extended, shall force conviction upon the world that Christianity is divine.[27]

Jesus' followers, in oneness with the Trinity and each other, present an undeniable light to the world that nothing else can approximate.

Verse 22: "The glory that you have given me I have given them, so that they may be one, as we are one,"

Jesus has already acted to enable His followers to be one. How? He said he gave His disciples glory—the glory that the Father gave to him. What did he mean by this? Jesus began this prayer with a request for the restoration of the glory that he had

---

[26] Ibid.

[27] R. Jamieson, A. R. Fausset, & D. Brown, *Commentary Critical and Explanatory on the Whole Bible* (Oak Harbor, WA: Logos Research Systems, Inc. 1997) (Jn 17:21).

enjoyed with the Father in eternity before creation. Then, late in the prayer he spoke of "the glory that you have given me." I do not believe that John has Jesus contradicting himself. This glory that the Father had given him was not the same as the glory that he requested to be restored to him. So, what glory had the Father given him? Let's explore that question.

"**The glory**": John had written that the disciples had seen Jesus' glory, "the glory of the One and Only" (John 1:14). When Jesus turned water into wine, he "revealed His glory" (John 2:11) to His disciples who witnessed this "sign" that led them to believe him. The glory that they saw was not a shining face or radiant clothing; Jesus looked ordinary to their eyes. It was the glory of God within him that was "full of grace and truth" (John 1:14) that they saw. How would it be to experience a human who always told the truth and whose life always conveyed absolute truthfulness? Is a fully gracious human being extraordinary? Of course! That is what to them Jesus looked like, and oh, so much more! Inwardly, God's glory in him was evident, from time to time showing up in a sign that they interpreted as a divine act. This unique glory, as well as the glory to be restored, could not be the glory Jesus spoke of as given to him from the Father and given by him to the disciples.

What was this glory that the Father gave to Jesus and Jesus gave to the disciples? Walvoord and Zuck suggest: "**The glory** which Christ **gave** the church may refer to the glory of the Cross."[28] Perhaps, but I am not sure that John directly answered this question. However, John's Gospel does record the testimony of John the Baptist that he saw the Holy Spirit descend upon Jesus at His baptism thereby identifying him as "the Son of God" (John 1:32-34). Is this an indirect reference to Jesus being given glory from heaven? Although John does not seem to provide an explicit answer, Peter wrote, "For he received honor and glory from God the Father when the voice came to him from the Majestic Glory" (2 Peter 1:17). Peter referred to Jesus'

---

[28] Blum, E. A., J. F. Walvoord & R. B. Zuck, eds, *The Bible Knowledge Commentary: An Exposition of the Scriptures* "John" (Wheaton, IL: Victor Books, 1985) (Jn 17:22–23).

transfiguration, detailed elsewhere in the Gospel accounts (Matthew 17:5; Mark 9:7; Luke 9:35). Previously in Jesus' life at his baptism, this voice spoke the same words spoken at the Transfiguration as the Holy Spirit descended. If this is the glory to which Jesus referred, then we can understand that through the Holy Spirit His followers through all time would share it.

John recorded Jesus speaking in present tense of future outcomes before they became reality in the present. One example is in John 7:37-39, where John as the narrator edits, "By this he meant the Spirit, whom those who believed in him were later to receive. Up to that time the Spirit had not been given, since Jesus had not yet been glorified." Jesus was speaking about what was to occur starting with the Pentecost ten days after His ascension. But he spoke of living waters flowing within believers as if it were a present reality. In his prayer, Jesus seemed to make similar statements about future realities as if they were present. Speaking of glory, he said, "I have given them," but he was referring to believers who had not yet become believers. If we confine Jesus' statements to the general rules of grammar and tense, we will misunderstand.

I believe that Jesus' next words offer us a clue about the glory of which he spoke. **"So that they may be one, as we are one"**: Whatever this glory was, it would enable His followers to be one as are he and the Father. He had requested the same for His disciples who were with him then (John 17:11). Through the protection that Jesus provided while with them (John 18:8-9), these disciples remained a unified group even through their fears and denials (John 20:19; 18:17, 25-26) after Jesus' arrest. However, their togetherness was not comparable with the oneness of the Trinity. How much more is that true of the fractured Church since. The next chapter gives more historic information about the Church. But, did Jesus put a time stamp on **when** this oneness—as of the Trinity—would be actualized? I believe that to understand we must consider Jesus' words in full context, and that includes what he continued to pray.

<u>Verse 23</u>: "I in them and you in me, that they may become completely one, so that the world may know that you have sent me and have loved them even as you have loved me."

Here Jesus describes **how** he gives His followers glory, and through it oneness in them. "**I in them**": At the time of this prayer, Jesus was not "in" any of His disciples. Previously that evening, he had promised them that the Father "will give you another Advocate, to be with you forever... the Spirit of truth... You know him, because he abides with you, and he will be in you. I will not leave you orphaned; I am coming to you" (John 14:16–18 *NRSV*). Who had been their Advocate?[29] Jesus. Who was abiding with them? Jesus. Who would not leave them orphaned? Jesus. His indwelling of His disciples would be possible through the Holy Spirit yet to be given.

"**You in me**": In the same conversation that Jesus told them about the indwelling Advocate through whom he would be in them, he said, "the Father who dwells in me does his works" (John 14:10). In this prayer, Jesus points to the Father indwelling him as the complement of His indwelling the disciples, and all through His ministry he had insisted that the Father in him did the work of ministry (John 5:19; 10:37-38; 14:10-12). His disciples would eventually understand that they could fulfill this otherwise human impossibility by the indwelling presence of Jesus through the Holy Spirit. Irenaeus put it this way:

> Wherefore also the Lord promised to send the Comforter, who should join us to God. For as a compacted lump of dough cannot be formed of dry wheat without fluid matter, nor can a loaf

---

[29] I. Howard Marshall, *New Testament Theology* (Downers Grove, IL: InterVarsity Press, 2004), 507. "the Spirit... takes on the task of Jesus as 'another' Paraclete. The term is used in 1 John 2:1."

possess unity, so, in like manner, neither could we, being many, be made one in Christ Jesus without the water from heaven.[30]

"That they may become completely one": Ah, now it becomes clear how oneness in humans can exist. On their own, they could not be one, but with Christ in them, they were to grow in unity and become completely one. The NASB with its marginal note reads "that they may be perfected into one." Note that both translations use passive construction of the phrase. It is not the growth of individual members or any grouping of members—local congregation, denomination, or otherwise—that results in oneness. It is accomplished solely by the indwelling presence of Jesus through the Holy Spirit.

Does this state represent the spiritual perfection of the Church and its members? John used *teleioo* in passive-verb form to describe the condition the NASB translated "perfected into one." The same word is found in Hebrews 12:23, where it speaks of "the spirits of the righteous made perfect." In both instances, the perfecting or completing work is done to the Church members, not by them. The meaning of *teleioo* does not imply intrinsic spiritual perfection like the sinless character of Jesus Christ, because it is applied to imperfect humans in whom God is at work. To more clearly understand the state of these Church members, we will look at a similar application of the base of this word, *teleios*, in Chapter 5.

"So that the world may know that you have sent me": This seems to be repetition of Jesus' request just two verses earlier. Perhaps it is. In prayer and conversations, we repeat ourselves. But when words or messages are written, repetition tends to be less common. So why did John repeat Jesus' words? The difference in the second request is that it is predicated on Jesus' followers becoming "completely one." Perhaps, through this repetition, John is emphasizing that convincing the world only

---

[30] Irenaeus, *Against Heresies* Book III.17:2.

occurs when the work of the Trinity in bringing about oneness in Jesus' followers is complete or perfected.

"And have loved them even as you have loved me": In addition to convincing the world that God the Father sent Jesus, the world needs to see the love of God that is the reason for this sending. This love is first for Jesus, but Jesus said that it is also for those Jesus sent. Amazingly, Jesus compares this love of the Father for the disciples to the Father's love for him!

In fact, evangelization is incomplete otherwise. Those who have rejected God and do not believe the gospel are in a disposition of hatred toward both the Father and the Son (John 15:23). Bluntly, they do not know God (John 15:21). For the same reason they hate those who believe in and follow Jesus (John 14:18; 17:14). Nonbelievers will be shocked to discover that those who they despised, rejected, and ridiculed were the "real deal"—sent from God.

Conclusion of the prayer (17:24-26): As he began, Jesus concluded his prayer with words that express the depth of his love. We can relate to his desire to be with those that he loves because we desire the same. His followers through all time are to be with him and see him in His glory forever. This love started with the love between the Father and Son in eternity, and now—Jesus concludes—these believers are participants. Because this includes groups in both part one and part two of the prayer, I did not include verses 24-26 in the above analysis. I am not alone in viewing these verses as the prayer's conclusion. The authors of the *New Bible Commentary* wrote: "The concluding verses (24–26) follow on from v. 24 but also form a fitting climax to the whole prayer."[31] The concluding words summarize this prayer: "that the love you have for me may be in them and that I myself may be in them." What a fabulous outcome to Jesus' self-sacrificing ministry! God's love for his One and Only shared with those that follow him, bringing together the whole family in mutually-shared oneness.

---

[31] D. A. Carson, et al., ed., *New Bible Commentary: 21st Century Edition* (Leicester, England; Downers Grove, IL: Inter-Varsity Press, 1994, 4th ed.), 1060.

I believe the written words recorded in John 17 cannot possibly convey the intensity of what Jesus uttered to His Father. In all of His life—a life full of prayer—Jesus had never before encountered this circumstance. He therefore poured out these profound words. A little over a decade ago, before the U.S. stock market crash, an advertising firm coined the expression, "When Merrill Lynch speaks, people listen." I suggest rephrasing the expression: "When Jesus prays, his followers listen." His prayer deserves our utmost attention. In the presence of his disciples and preserved for us, he bared the heart of God about the essentiality of oneness with the Trinity founded on love. Yes, Lord! And yes, Holy Spirit, for John 17 is not the only inspired New Testament passage about oneness.

Related Passages

John, in his Gospel and his three epistles, emphasizes the themes of love and oneness more than any New Testament writer. But his teaching is not unique. Paul's writing style distinguishes him from John, but the two share the emphasis on oneness and love. Paul writes about the outworking of Jesus' prayer in the life of the Church. One example, but not the only is in the fourth chapter of Ephesians.

Paul preached the gospel in Ephesus on his third missionary journey (Acts 18:18-19:20). Through his preaching there, many Jews and Greeks throughout the province of Asia believed (Acts 19:10, 18-20). Congregations emerged, including in Ephesus, a racially and culturally mixed city. Unlike the members of the Jewish Synagogue, which consisted of Jews and Gentile proselytes—more than one race but one culture—the Church accepted members, including uncircumcised Gentiles, without attempting to change their culture. This made the church at Ephesus a blend of peoples and cultures. Paul pastored that congregation for two years. Some years later, when Paul was imprisoned in Rome, he wrote the letter to the saints at Ephesus, intended as a circular letter for the churches of the whole Roman province of Asia.[32]

He wrote about the marvelous grace that God had granted them in calling them to be His adopted children (Ephesians 1:5-6). He said that God the Father had given them every gift in the heavenly realm. He went on to elaborate on the details of these gifts and what they meant to them, and through the preservation of his letter in Scripture, to all Christians.[33] According to D. A. Carson and his associates, the theme of the letter is cosmic reconciliation in Christ. They wrote:

> All this could be called cosmic reconciliation. Ephesians teaches that this purpose has been begun in Christ and will be consummated in him. In him alienation has been destroyed and unification begun: the old division of humanity into Jew and Gentile has been overcome (2:10-16); and the older alienation of humankind from God surmounted too (2:17-18). Christ has begun to 'fill' and unite the universe (4:10), bringing peace. But to say these things have begun in him is also to say they are experienced by those united with him, namely by believers.[34]

Thus, the theme of oneness in Christ with God and with each other, regardless of our various identities as humans, is deeply woven throughout this letter. Paul's teaching style portrays what oneness in the Church looks like. He addresses the characteristics of oneness in a local congregation as well as factors that hinder a local congregation from being one. Let us look at a summary of his teachings in the fourth chapter.

---

[32] Carson, et al., 1222.

[33] Ibid., (4:7-12).

[34] Carson, et al., 1223.

Ephesians 4:1-16

V. 1-3: Paul urged his readers to lead a life worthy of their calling, that is, in the context of being in a called-out group of believers. Michael J. Gorman wrote: "the church, which is richly blessed in Christ, dwells as a community of Gentiles and Jews... as one body with different gifts, but with a common ethic of compassion, respect, and holiness."[35] These first few verses present a high-level image of a how the local congregations to which Paul wrote were to look.[36] Unity and love are foundational.

V. 4-6: Paul's Greek includes words that are translated seven times as "one" in most English translations.[37] John had used a form of these words five times in Jesus' prayer.[38] The repetition and emphases are inescapable. If oneness prevails in the Church, the Holy Spirit, hope, Jesus, faith, baptism, and the Father, how can we be in anything short of this oneness?

V. 7-11: Though we are one Church, that Church consists of members with a diversity of gifts. God is the author of this diversity. Paul uses the analogy of the body with its parts, as he does in detail in the verses that follow, to emphasize oneness with diversity.

V. 12-16: The purpose of this diversity of gifts is the growth and wholeness of the Church. The list of spiritual gifts mentioned

---

[35] Michael J. Gorman, *Reading Paul* (Eugene, OR: Cascade Books, 2008), 37.

[36] Carson, et. al., commenting on the use of "one" in V. 4-6 adds: "It is worth noting that all this addresses unity both within the local congregation and, more especially, as a universal church. Many Christians have often been more keen to promote the loving harmony of a single congregation (even sometimes, alas, only of cliques within it!) than to deal with the divisions between churches" (1237).

[37] Robertson, on Eph. 4:4-5. "**One body** (ἐν σωμα [*hen sōma*])... **One Spirit** (ἐν πνευμα [*hen pneuma*])... **In one hope** (ἐν μιᾳ ἐλπιδι [*en miāi elpidi*])... **One Lord** (εἰς Κυριος [*heis Kurios*]). **One faith** (μια πιστις [*mia pistis*])... **One baptism** (ἐν βαπτισμα [*hen baptisma*])... **One God and Father of all** (εἰς θεος και πατηρ παντων [*heis theos kai patēr pantōn*])."

[38] Robertson, on John 17. "Each time Jesus uses ἐν [*hen*] (verses 11, 21, 22) and once, εἰς ἐν [*eis hen*], 'into one' (verse 23)."

here is not an exhaustive list. There are others as shown in Romans 12, 1 Corinthians 12, and elsewhere in the New Testament. The gifts mentioned specifically relate to equipping the Church for ministry toward growing it to maturity in knowledge and application. As Paul put it in 12–15 (*NRSV*):

> Until all of us come to the unity of the faith and of the knowledge of the Son of God, to maturity, to the measure of the full stature of Christ. We must no longer be children, tossed to and fro and blown about by every wind of doctrine, by people's trickery, by their craftiness in deceitful scheming. But speaking the truth in love, we must grow up in every way into him who is the head, into Christ.

Paul's "maturity" is based on *telos* as in John 17:23, where it is translated "perfected" in the NASB.[39] Paul continues, using the human body as an example of the Church. Each member: organ, muscle, ligament, bone, artery, vein, nerve, tube has a part in the wholeness, health, and strength of the body. Paul describes the body as a growing organism. To be healthy and fully functional, all parts must grow together. The analogy presents an elaboration on the concept of oneness in Jesus Christ. Paul, in his teaching that follows in the remainder of the letter details the attitudes and behaviors that are manifestations of this oneness.

Manifestations of Oneness in the Church

We have seen that the oneness for which Jesus prayed is characterized by self-giving love: between the Father and Jesus, between Jesus and His followers, and in His followers for one another. Love itself has manifestations as Paul beautifully described in 1 Corinthians 13. Similarly, the oneness for which

---

[39] See the footnote about the NRSV words "completely one" in the explanation of John 17:23.

Jesus prayed has manifestations. Noticeable manifestations of this oneness include, but are not limited to, common faith, hope, and baptism as Paul mentioned. In oneness, we believe the same, hope in the same, and are baptized into the same—Father Son, and Spirit. When church members are one in Christ, they share warm fellowship, they serve each other, and they worship together as one as Michael Jinkins explained[40] and as Paul wrote to the saints in Philippi (Philippians 2:1-4):

> Therefore if you have any encouragement from being united with Christ, if any comfort from his love, if any common sharing in the Spirit, if any tenderness and compassion, then make my joy complete by being like-minded, having the same love, being one in spirit and of one mind. Do nothing out of selfish ambition or vain conceit. Rather, in humility value others above yourselves, not looking to your own interests but each of you to the interests of the others.

The oneness for which Jesus prayed unifies believers in many ways. Unity is a beautiful thing, but in music, harmony (unity with diversity) is even more beautiful. We can produce unity and harmony as well as teamwork in our human endeavors, such as music ensembles, sports teams, and even work groups. But I believe that the oneness for which Jesus prayed is greater than all these and cannot be produced by human ability. Why? Because that oneness stems from the oneness of the Trinity. I believe that, in the context of the Church, unity, union, harmony, fellowship, togetherness, relational love, friendship, love-union, and community are all manifestations of oneness in the Trinity.

---

[40] See his use of *koinonia, diakonia,* and *leitourgia* cited in this book's Appendix.

-4-

Has Church Lived Up?

Jesus prayed for oneness in the Church, but has his prayer been answered? Nearly 2000 years of Church history tells the story of both success and failure among His followers. Success, really? one might ask. Yes, when we understand exactly what Jesus expected in the answer. His own words clearly suggest a process of growth toward "complete" or "perfect" oneness (John 17:23). Paul wrote about the same subject, using the Greek word *teleios* translated as "mature" to describe this process (Ephesians 4:13).

Because the history of the Church is a subject far too big for even a summary in this book, I will select a small number of historical examples that illustrate both successes and failures. My purpose is to illustrate that history validates that at times, and in less than perfect ways, Jesus' prayer for oneness has been answered. At the same time, admitting reality, I intend to cite a sample of historical Church failures to live in oneness. As in all failures, admitting them is the first step toward correcting them. In the next chapter I hope to harness some of the lessons of failure to encourage our application of Jesus' intent of oneness in the Church, because this marvelous prayer of Jesus is yet to be *teleios*—fulfilled.

The First Century Church

Our starting point is with the twelve apostles and those who complemented them in evangelizing their part of the world and nurturing the Church. Immediately, we can observe a remarkable fact: history does not record any major division or schism among the twelve original apostles and those later designated apostles, such as Barnabas and Paul (Acts 14:14).

Luke[41], generally considered the author of the book of Acts, described the Church in Jerusalem in the initial year after it was formed: "All the believers were one in heart and mind" (Acts 4:32). But, make no mistake, Luke also wrote of problems that arose, for example: "In those days when the number of the disciples was increasing, the Grecian Jews among them complained against the Hebraic Jews" (Acts 6:1). But in resolving these problems the Apostles exhibited the standard of oneness that Jesus had set, and the Church members followed suit (6:2-6), and as Luke added, "So the word of God spread" (6:7). As time went on, an issue arose about Peter's association with Gentiles, consequently some Church members "criticized him" (Acts 11:2). That problem too was resolved with "no further objections" (11:18).

As the Church became more diverse, stronger disagreements arose. An incident at the Church in Antioch exposed a simmering disagreement among church leaders. Luke wrote, "This brought Paul and Barnabas into sharp dispute and debate with them" (Acts 15:2). Clearly, resolution guided by the Holy Spirit was needed. Luke continued the story, detailing how at the initiative of local church members, Paul and Barnabas traveled to Jerusalem to meet with the Apostles and church leaders, who convened a council that, guided by the Holy Spirit, effectively worked together to preserve Church oneness (15:3-6, 28).

The Apostles were not immune to mistakes that jeopardized Church oneness. The letter to the Galatians mentions a case in which church leaders erred in judgment, and actions resulted in conflict between Peter and Paul, who wrote "I opposed him to his face" (Galatians 2:11). But they recovered to preserve oneness (2:12-15). Although Paul did not say here that Peter agreed, this

---

[41] Robert L. Gallagher and Paul Hertig, *Mission in Acts* (Maryknoll, NY:Orbis Books, 2006), 8. "Some scholars argue that Luke-Acts was written to non-Christians as an apologetic... Within this overarching purpose are many other subtopics, such as the unity of the flourishing movement within diversity, in spite of tensions and setbacks. Furthermore, Acts provided assurance to political leaders that Christianity was not a threat to Rome."

dispute seems to highlight the authority of the word of God in resolving differences, and the courage as well as humility in leaders willing to preserve oneness while correcting wrongs.

On the other hand, there were disputes about matters that did not fall into the category of right verses wrong. Luke records the disagreement between Paul and Barnabas about the involvement of Mark in the ministry of the gospel. "They had such a sharp disagreement that they parted company" (Acts 15:36-39). Their team, previously commissioned by inspiration of the Holy Spirit (Acts 13:2), split; however, their split did not divide the Church or the ministry of the gospel, and later correspondence confirmed that their relationship remained intact (1 Corinthians 9:6). Also, the split resulted in multiplied missionary teams.

Christian scholars have speculated about the relationship between Paul and James, the brother of Jesus, suspecting that the two might have been adversaries. Allegedly, they were at odds about their teachings on faith and justification, but Tremper Longman III and David E. Garland challenge such speculation:

> Some have suggested that Paul and James were ministering and thinking independently, and that their writings reflect no interaction one with the other. Yet we know from Galatians and Acts (Gal 1:19; 2:9 Ac. 15; 21:17-26) that they had significant interaction. This... makes this position unlikely.[42]

Paul and James are to me excellent examples of ministers of Jesus Christ who could easily oppose each other if they disregarded Jesus' prayer to be one. The two men had very different assignments in the early church. James served in Jerusalem; Paul served in Gentile areas (Acts 21:17-20). The cultures differed widely, and tensions between the two cultures were high. Nonetheless, the narrative in Acts 21 exhibits the

---

[42] Tremper Longman III and David E. Garland, *The Expositors Bible Commentary: Hebrews – Revelation*, (Grand Rapids, MI: Zondervan, 2006) 42.

respect and love—instead of animosity—that these two men shared toward each other.

In spite of the oneness exhibited in the apostles, eventually the first-century Church showed signs of significant fragmenting. In Paul's first letter to the church in Corinth, he urged them "in the name of our Lord Jesus Christ, that all of you agree with one another so that there may be no divisions among you" (1 Corinthians 1:10). He added in the same letter, "there are divisions among you" (11:18-19). Elsewhere, schisms became such a widespread threat that Paul warned of them in his speech to the church leaders in Ephesus (Acts 20:29-30). He included similar warnings in his pastoral letters to Timothy and Titus (1 Timothy 1:3; 2 Timothy 2:17-18; 4:3; Titus 1:10-11). Even the congregation in Philippi that excelled in supporting Paul's ministry (Philippians 4:15) suffered from an internal rivalry (4:2). Later letters from Peter, John, and Jude dealt with even deeper divisions springing from heresy (2 Peter 2:1-2; 1 John 2:19; 3:7; 4:1; 2 John 7-10; 3 John 9-10; Jude 4, 8-19).

The writings of the Ante-Nicene Fathers confirm that schisms continued to spread in the early Church. Ignatius, Bishop of Antioch, who was born in the first half of the first century and died shortly after the close of it, placed heavy emphasis on the congregational members' relationship with, and respect for, their Bishop.[43] I believe that this emphasis was to counter the many heretics who were trying to mislead the church members to gain a following. Ignatius summed it this way in one letter: "where the shepherd is, there do ye as sheep follow. For there are many wolves that appear worthy of credit, who, by means of a pernicious pleasure, carry captives those that are running towards God."[44] Using the metaphor of music with instruments and choir together producing song to God through Jesus Christ, Ignatius

---

[43]Ignatius, *Ephesians* V, *Magnesians* III, *Trallians* II, *Philadelphians* II, Philip Schaff, ed., *The Apostolic Fathers with Justin Martyr and Irenaeus,* III.1.1 *Ante-Nicene Fathers* Vol. 1.

[44] Ignatius, *Phildephians* II.

described the oneness desired and expected in each congregation.[45] His letters demonstrate that the Church was struggling to maintain this oneness.

The Church After the First Century

Irenaeus, Bishop of Lyons, France in the late second century, wrote five known books titled *Against Heresies*. By then, church leaders' intense fight against division and heresy rose to such a high level that many of the written records that have been preserved for us to study are devoted to refuting heretical teachings. Consequently, these writings do not paint a complete picture of the Church. Irenaeus' writings are a case in point. Nonetheless, despite his abhorrence of heresies and opposition to the heretics, he wrote about the oneness of belief and teaching in the Church, regardless of location or language:

> She [the Church] also believes... as if she had but one soul, and one and the same heart, and she proclaims them, and teaches them, and hands them down, with perfect harmony, as if she possessed only one mouth. For although the languages of the world are dissimilar, yet the import of the tradition is one and the same. For the churches that have been planted in Germany do not believe or hand down anything different.[46]

This oneness that Irenaeus observed was not enforced by the Roman government, which at that time remained opposed to Christianity. Being so widespread, it could not have been the result of control of a bishop or group of bishops. The logical conclusion is that this oneness was in the leaders and members of the Church.

---

[45] Ibid., *Ephesians* IV.

[46] Irenaeus, *Against Heresies* (I.X.2).

Eusebius, a fourth-century Christian historian, wrote about the peace experienced in the Church throughout the Roman Empire during Emperor Constantine's reign: "Mutual love was exhibited between people, the members of Christ's body were united in complete harmony."[47] Eusebius saw more in the Church than agreement on teachings. He continued: "And there was one energy of the Divine Spirit pervading all the members, and one soul in all, and the same eagerness of faith, and one hymn from all in praise of the Deity."[48] No doubt, this condition was facilitated by Constantine's authority and actions to relieve Christians of persecution.[49] But authority does not force people to love each other. Perhaps some degree of the oneness and harmony expressed in the church members was an outcome of reduced schisms within. However, the primary factor, according to Eusebius' quote above about "one energy of the Divine Spirit," was the oneness through the Holy Spirit in the members.

In the fourth century, Constantine also tried to bring the clerical factions of the Church together in unity. As a political leader and ruler, his methods involved use of his authority with enforcement as necessary.[50] This, of course, was not Jesus' intent.

Through the years, the Church has attempted to unify itself through similar means. But, again, whether a bishop or the

---

[47] Eusebius, *The Church History of Eusebius*, (X.III.1). *Nicene and Post Nicene Fathers* Series 2, Vol.1, Philip Schaff, ed.

[48] Ibid, X.III.2.

[49] Ibid, X.II.1. About the effect of these actions, Eusebius recorded: "All men, then, were freed from the oppression of the tyrants, and being released from the former ills, one in one way and another in another acknowledged the defender of the pious to be the only true God. And we especially who placed our hopes in the Christ of God had unspeakable gladness, and a certain inspired joy bloomed for all of us, when we saw every place which shortly before had been desolated by the impieties of the tyrants reviving as if from a long and death-fraught pestilence, and temples again rising from their foundations to an immense height, and receiving a splendor far greater than that of the old ones which had been destroyed."

[50] Gonzalez, Kindle location 3348. "The Empire had a vested interest in the unity of the church, which Constantine hoped would become the 'cement of the Empire'."

Bishop of Rome—the pope—or a self-proclaimed apostle, no such attempts succeeded. All were based on the premise of hierarchical authority versus oneness expressing the love of God through the indwelling of the Holy Spirit.

Some attempts at unity were seemingly well intentioned. One such attempt arose when the growth of local churches resulted in multiple congregations in the same community. About the church's response, Justo Gonzalez wrote:

> The unity of the body of Christ was so important that it seemed that something was lost when in a single city there were several congregations. In order to preserve and symbolize the bond of unity, the custom arose in some places to send a piece of bread from the communion served in the bishop's church—the 'fragmentum'—to be added to the bread to be used in other churches.[51]

As the first-century Church resolved a major disagreement through the council that Luke wrote about in Acts 15, later church leaders convened councils to resolve disagreements and foster unity. In several of these cases, the outcomes of the councils were agreement by the majority to endorse a particular doctrine, such as the doctrine of the Trinity in 381 at Constantinople[52] and the doctrine of the nature of Jesus in 451 at Chalcedon.[53] A brief summary of seven of these councils is in the following table:

---

[51] Gonzalez, Kindle location 2203.

[52] Spickard and Cragg, 107.

[53] Ibid.

Nicaea – 325 AD	Resolved the dispute over Arianism, the heretical teaching that Jesus Christ is not truly God. Issued the Nicene Creed
Constantinople – 381 AD	Resolved the dispute over Apollinarianism, the heretical teaching that Jesus Christ was God but not human in mind. Revised the Nicene Creed.
Ephesus – 431 AD	Resolved the dispute over Nestorianism, the heretical teaching that Jesus Christ's two natures—human and divine—were separate and thus not both subject to suffering.
Chalcedon – 451 AD	Further defined Jesus Christ's nature to resolve controversies. Issued the Chalcedon Creed.
Constantinople II – 553 AD	Addressed further disputes about the nature of Jesus Christ, agreeing with the view of the Eastern Church that emphasized the divine nature over the human nature.
Constantinople III – 680 AD	Correction of the Eastern Church's view of Jesus Christ's nature that was established in the previous council, affirming the reality of two wills in Christ.
Nicaea – 787 AD	Overturned the decisions in 754 AD against the use of icons in matters of worship

These councils succeeded in keeping the oneness of the faith and doctrine in the churches. Through them the Church in the East and West, through most of the first millennium after Christ, continued in a unified approach to teachings about God, Jesus

Christ, and the Trinity. In each case, a heretical teaching was identified as such and rejected, resulting in the disassociation of the individual or group that held to it. Perhaps the most influential result of the councils was the issuance of a creedal document agreed to by an overwhelming majority of the Bishops in attendance. Later in this chapter, we will consider details on two of these creeds that today continue to shape most churches today.

Although some of these councils resulted in unified teachings, no council brought about Church oneness according to the standard of Jesus' prayer—oneness not just in identical beliefs and teachings but in relationship.

Many of the early schisms in the Church were the result of differences between church leaders about the application of loving forgiveness of the "lapsed"—those who sinned in noticeable ways, such as known sexual acts and defections from the faith under persecution. Donatism sought to separate the "pure" from the "apostate" Church.[54] About these, Gonzalez wrote,

> The significance of these episodes is that they show that the restoration of the lapsed was one of the main concerns of the Western Church from a very early date. The question of what should be done about those baptized Christians who sinned divided the Western Church repeatedly.[55]

Other schisms occurred for the most ridiculous reasons. For example, a division among Eastern Orthodox Christians in Russia from their Greek counterparts would be laughable if its implications were not so serious. The two parties quarreled and split over the number of fingers to wave while making the sign of the cross. As Spickard and Cragg wrote:

---

[54] Ibid., Kindle location 3273.

[55] Ibid., Kindle location 2112.

The schism occurred over a seemingly trivial matter of hand signals. Nicon tried to get Russian Christians, who had been enthusiastic supporters of Avvakum's reforms, to abandon the practice of making the sign of the cross with two fingers, and substitute instead the Greek use of three fingers.[56]

The most notable split in Church history divided the Eastern Christians from the Western. Spickard and Cragg wrote: "The Eastern and Western churches split apart formally in 1054. The issues of the moment were a dispute over the authority of the pope and a theological argument about the *filioque* clause."[57] There were genuine issues that needed resolution. As Gonzalez points out, the two major branches of the Church had been drifting apart for some time, but it was the inability of two church leaders to act out the oneness for which Jesus prayed that gives this split an air of outrageous disharmony. Instead of seeking oneness and at least trying to negotiate about the differences, Cardinal Humbart, representing Pope Leo IX and Eastern Church Patriarch, Michael Cerularuis met and mutually excommunicated each other.[58]

Then, there was the *great schism* over the elections of popes in 1378. As a result, "Half of Europe's church leaders accepted Clement VII, while the other half remained loyal to the pope at Rome."[59] This type of feud is common in political circles, and

---

[56] Spickard and Cragg, 117.

[57] Spickard and Cragg, 110. "The *filioque* debate... surrounded the original and proper wording of the Nicene Creed. Eastern Christians accused their Roman counterparts of changing the creed to fit their political expediency. Western Christians denied the charge. For nearly two hundred years, from 858 to 1054, controversy on the subject waxed and waned."

[58] Gonzalez, Kindle location 5448.

[59] Ibid., 150.

when the Western Church in medieval Europe delved into politics it found itself in the same predicament.

The Protestant Reformation, initiated by Martin Luther in 1517, resulted in a dramatic split between the reformers who supported him and the Roman Catholic Church.[60] Subsequently, in 1555 according to Spickard and Cragg, the *Peace of Augsburg* "marked official recognition that the split between Protestant and Catholic had permanently broken the Body of Christ apart."[61] However, this split was not over trivial matters. The reformers were convinced that the papal-led church had drastically strayed from everything that the Church of Jesus Christ was about.[62]

Although divisions of such magnitude appear to be Church problems, God only knows to what extent the real battle was between believers or between believers and spirit enemies of God. Paul encountered such enemy assaults in his time, and wrote the following about them: "For our struggle is not against flesh and blood, but against the powers of this dark world and against the spiritual forces of evil in the heavenly realms (Ephesians 6:12)." On record, such struggles appear to be between human parties in the Church instead of the demonic impetus that can be the real cause.

Carson, et al. comment on the Church's historical record: "If we pause to reflect on the church's record of disunity, we can easily see how far we have fallen short of Jesus' requirements."[63]

The small number of examples of oneness compared to the many examples of schisms in the Church through the past two millennia indeed convicts the Church that it has fallen short of fulfilling Jesus' prayer. My intention in citing this comparison is not to advocate a movement to stir the Church into action. Instead, I am echoing Jesus' prayer and what it means to the Church. Jesus, through the Holy Spirit, is fully capable of

---

[60] Ibid., 177.

[61] Ibid., 180.

[62] Johnson and Webber, 358.

[63] D. A. Carson, et al., 1060.

awakening the Church to hear and trust him to be able to heed his words.

History attributes these many failures and relatively few successes to "the Church." But how much of what is recorded really stemmed from the Church? Peter noted that "their shameful ways will bring the way of truth into disrepute" (2 Peter 2:2). Those to whom he referred were false prophets and teachers. Their actions reflected on the reputation of the Church, although they were imposters. About similar individuals, John wrote, "They went out from us, but they did not really belong to us" (1 John 2:19). Jesus had likened them to weeds sowed by the enemy in the field of good wheat, and He added that they will not be separated from the recognized assembly of His chosen wheat until the harvest (Matthew 13:24-30). Since this was the state of the Church even in the first century, when it was small and still led by the apostles, how much more has it been since! According to these biblical revelations, false representations of the Church could be littering history, so that the real fulfillment of Jesus' prayer is difficult to discern from the outside looking into the Church. Calvin's theory of the visible and invisible Church proposes an explanation. Alister McGrath wrote that Calvin taught: "At one level, the Church is the community of Christian believers, a visible group. It is also, however, the fellowship of saints and the company of the elect, known only to God."[64] McGrath continues to quote Calvin, explaining that the visible Church as seen by historic as well as contemporary eyes, "includes both good and evil, elect and reprobate."[65] This theory is consistent with Yahweh's statement to Elijah the prophet, when Elijah complained: "The Israelites have rejected your covenant, broken down your altars, and put your prophets to death with the sword. I am the only one left." To this, the God of Israel responded: "I reserve seven thousand in Israel—all of whose

---

[64] Alister E. McGrath, *Christian Theology and Introduction* (Malden, MA: Blackwell Publishers, 1994), 469.

[65] Ibid.

knees have not bowed down to Baal" (1 Kings 19:14, 18). There was then a visible but unfaithful Israel as well as the invisible faithful smaller group. I agree with Calvin's view that the same is true of the Church.

Whether a result of spiritual attacks or faults among believers, these high-profile historical examples of disunity and disharmony portray the Church as a type of photo-negative—the exact opposite of the oneness for which Jesus prayed. Is that where the story of the Church ends? I don't think so. Otherwise, I would have no reason to write this book. There is more to tell than the failures of recorded history.

The Creeds

The Prophet Amos wrote in 3:3, "Do two walk together unless they have agreed to do so?" Amos' inspired question simply states a vital principle of oneness: regardless of the endeavor, two cannot be one unless something between them allows it, and an important something is agreement. The great creeds, about which Catholics, Orthodox[66], and Protestants have agreed for almost 2000 years is an example of doctrinal and theological oneness in the Church.

Creeds were a part of the Church's expression of agreement from the beginning. First-Century Church members expressed their choice of Jesus' lordship over Caesar's with the creed, "Jesus is Lord" (1 Corinthians 12:3; Philippians 2:11). In the fourth Century, teachings that differed from those commonly held led the Church to the first major creed as a result of the Council of Nicaea in 325 AD. The Nicene-Constantinopolitan creed, a revision in 381 AD of the Nicene Creed by the Council of Constantinople, remains today, along with the Apostle's Creed, as unifying statements of common beliefs that span the Christian world. Frances M. Young wrote, "Christianity is the only major religion to set such store by creeds."[67] It is indeed commendable

---

[66] With the exception of the *filioque* debate mentioned previously.

[67] Frances M Young, *The Making of the Creeds* (London: SCM Press, 1991), 1.

that churches agree on their basic beliefs, the essential truths of Christianity: belief in one God in the Father, in Jesus Christ as Son of God and human, in the Holy Spirit, in the one universal Church, and in the communion of the saints, the forgiveness of sins, the resurrection, eternal life, and the return of Jesus. It is equally regrettable that these agreed-to beliefs seem to fall below the line of emphasis in matters of oneness in favor of less-important matters.

Oneness Among Humans is a Miracle

Although the Christian Scholars quoted in this chapter, and this author too, point out with regret and sadness that the Church has fallen short of the oneness for which Jesus prayed, their disappointment is not indicative of failure. It was not humanly possible for the Church to be one; only by a miraculous work of the triune God could it be achieved. That is exactly why Jesus prayed for it. If it was not a divinely appointed accomplishment, the world would not give it attention.

Consider Yahweh's promise to Abraham that his descendants would inherit the land of Canaan; that promise could only have been divinely fulfilled. Abraham had no descendants at the time of the promise, and he and Sara had to wait twenty five years after the promise was made—long after either naturally could have a child—for their child to be born.

When the God of Abraham, Isaac, and Jacob brought the enslaved Israelite nation—millions of Abraham's descendants through Isaac and Jacob—out of Egypt and led them into the promised land, the world, especially inhabitants of Egypt and the people resident in the land of Canaan, as well as all of the surrounding nations of the Middle East, all of them that witnessed the supernatural deliverance were awestruck. For a while, some actually believed in the one true God.

For the Church to live up to Jesus' prayer will be a similar miracle.

5

The Church's Echo

When I was five years old, my dad started to build a new shed at the back edge of our property. Curious as most five year olds, I enjoyed being with and watching my daddy as he worked. As I stood there, observing him putting up board after board, nailing them into place, surprisingly he said, "Martin, come here and help me put up this board." The board was large enough to be used as a support for what would become the roof. Dad placed the board on the floor where he wanted it and held it vertically; then he called me to get next to him and hold it. I did, rather loosely, as much as my less-than 50-pound body was able. "Hold it tight Martin," he said as he stepped up a ladder while continuing to hold the upper part of the board. To my tiny body, the board was so heavy and tall that I moved with every slight shift that it made as he scaled the ladder; that sparked an all-out effort in me to keep the board in place, but its weight was beyond my ability to hold it. Nonetheless, somehow I had reached the conclusion that if I did not hold that board well, it could fall and hurt my daddy. My grip was tight. "Hold it Martin," he urged, pulling out a large nail, somehow still holding the board near the top, continuing to encourage me, he nailed it into place. Then he came down and praised me for doing such a good job, feeding my pride in my accomplishment and importance to him.

Only later did I recall that feeling of sheer inability as I was holding the board, realizing then that my daddy had held nearly 100 percent, while I held not much more than zero percent. Although out of love for him and desire to please him, I had held it with all my might, my actual contribution to the job was nothing. But what an experience! My dad had allowed me to participate with him in building the shed, and he enjoyed my involvement. He loved me and wanted me to be with him. I loved him in return and wanted to be part of what he was doing. In that sense, we had shared oneness.

I had other siblings. If any of them would have been part of that experience, the same oneness would have been necessary. My eight-year-old brother could have held the board better than I. My sisters, 10 and 12, could have done even better. But for some reason Daddy chose me, although in reality he didn't need any of us to help him. The point is that he enjoyed my participation and I had fun with him. That moment was special because of the relational love between us, and the impression of that love remains on me to this day. If somehow I had refused this wonderful oneness, I could not have participated successfully in the work, and I would not have experienced this expression of my daddy's love for me. Imagine the result if one of my siblings and I had contended over holding the board and caused it to slip out of place. Although we were incapable of erecting it, we could have caused damage.

This true story illustrates the point of this chapter: our Father in heaven invites us to participate in his building project—not to build a shed, but the Body of Christ. He invites us through Jesus Christ and in the Holy Spirit to participate in this world-impacting project that directly involves the Church. God does not need us, but in love, wants us to be willing and cooperative participants in this project, necessitating our oneness with him and each other. That was the subject of the third part of Jesus' prayer.

Building Up the "Body"

Paul wrote in Ephesians 4:12, "so that the body of Christ may be built up." What did he mean? In the first chapter of this letter, Paul defined the body with these words in vv. 22-23: "God… appointed **him** to be head over everything for the **church, which is** his body." The "**him**" is Jesus Christ (1:20). As previously explained, Paul used the metaphor of a building to describe the Church as a work in progress (Ephesians 2:21). In a similar way, he used the metaphor of a body in Ephesians 4 to emphasize the organic nature of the Church and its many members.

We examined part of this chapter previously, but now we will analyze particularly vv. 11-16, paying close attention to the initiator of oneness, the response of the participants—church leaders and members, and the outcome within the Church.

> Christ himself gave the apostles, the prophets, the evangelists, the pastors and teachers, to equip his people for works of service, so that the body of Christ may be built up until we all reach unity in the faith and in the knowledge of the Son of God and become mature, attaining to the whole measure of the fullness of Christ. Then we will no longer be infants, tossed back and forth by the waves, and blown here and there by every wind of teaching and by the cunning and craftiness of people in their deceitful scheming. Instead, speaking the truth in love, we will grow to become in every respect the mature body of him who is the head, that is, Christ. From him the whole body, joined and held together by every supporting ligament, grows and builds itself up in love, as each part does its work.

Verse 11: "**Christ himself gave the apostles, the prophets, the evangelists, the pastors and teachers**": Jesus was directly involved with the Church from its inception and has continued. He chose the 12 apostles. After his ascension, he sent the Holy Spirit, filling the new Church in presence, with power, and through guidance to carry on in their mission. At the same time, as the book of Acts tells, Jesus Christ continued as head of the Church, choosing Saul of Tarsus who became Paul, bringing him to belief and obedience, and appearing purposefully at particular times to other leaders, such as James and Stephen.

Verse 12: "**to equip his people for works of service, so that the body of Christ may be built up**": These human leaders, gifted by the Holy Spirit, served then and continued afterward in different types of ministries to prepare the rest of the Church's gifted members for their ministry roles, all of which work together for the mutual growth—the building up of the whole Church. Like a well-trained, coordinated team of role players, synergistically contributing to, in effect, make the whole greater than the sum of its parts, these individuals contribute together organically for overall Church spiritual growth.

Verse 13: **"until we all reach unity in the faith and in the knowledge of the Son of God and become mature, attaining to the whole measure of the fullness of Christ."**: Notice the change in tense as this passage proceeds: Christ "gave" (past, active), leaders "equip" (present, active), the body of Christ "may be built" (present, passive), "until... reach" (future, passive). At the time of Paul's writing, Jesus had supplied the spiritual gifts, the Church was actively applying them, but the Church had not reached unity in maturity; I do not believe that the Church could claim that it reached that state at any time since. So, attaining to unity and maturity are still works-in-progress. "Unity" in Greek is ἑνότητα [*henotēta*], from the root ἕν [*hen*], the word John used for **"one"** in Jesus prayer. Robertson translates *henotēta* as "oneness."[68] The direction of growth in oneness is toward maturity. "Mature" in Greek is *teleios*, the root of the word that John used in Jesus' prayer (John 17:23) translated "completely" in the NRSV and "perfected" in the NASB. When this word is used in the context of spiritual growth, it applies to spiritual maturity. I make these technical points to show the relationship between Jesus' prayer and Paul's echo. (An echo is the repetition of reflected sounds or words.) Paul's words echo Jesus' prayer, redirecting the message to the readers of his letter, which explains in detail how the process of growth toward mature oneness takes place.

This growth in oneness involves first faith—trusting Jesus, and second knowing him. As the Church increases its absolute

---

[68] Archibald T. Robertson, *Word Pictures in the New Testament* (Nashville, TN: Broadman Press, 1933), Logos Software 4 on Eph. 4:13. **Unto the unity of the faith** (εἰς την ἑνότητα της πιστεως [*eis tēn henotēta tēs pisteōs*]). "Unto oneness of faith"

trust in Jesus, and no one or nothing else, and as members increasingly know Jesus, the whole body of believers matures. Like an aged but growing tree reaches complete height, ultimately the Church will reach full maturity, which is measured by the standard of Jesus Christ—full conformance to him to the extent of ultimately becoming like him in his humanity. At no time in history has this been achieved, in the same way that at no time in Paul's life of union in Christ had he attained perfection, or *teleioo* (Philippians 3:12). But Paul's intent was not a prophetic statement of some point in church history when complete oneness is attained. Rather, he wrote of a state or condition both he and the Church were to pursue (3:13-14). He even considered this attitude of ongoing pursuit an indication of spiritual maturity, at least, it seems, in a relative sense, prompting him to write, "All of us who are mature (*teleios*) should take such a view of things" (3:15).

Verse 14: "**Then we will no longer be infants, tossed back and forth by the waves, and blown here and there by every wind of teaching and by the cunning and craftiness of people in their deceitful scheming.**" Still in future tense, Paul describes spiritual maturity as the opposite of spiritual infanthood. Paul had written previously to another church in 1 Corinthians 3:1, "Brothers, I could not address you as spiritual but as worldly— mere infants in Christ." Although these church members were not new in the faith, they possessed few discernable differences from non-believers.

Perhaps the earliest memory of my childhood is of a baseball game at Memorial Stadium in Springfield, Ohio in the mid-to-late 1940s. I recall sitting on my grandmother's lap as she sat next to my mom in the grandstand behind home plate along the third base line. My mom was trying to tell me that Daddy was one of the players on the field, excitedly pointing in his direction, urging me to recognize him among the other players, but all I saw were players who looked alike, because they were all wearing the team uniform. In spite of my mom's pointing and urgings, I could not pick out my dad among the other players.

My mind, the mind of a child less than two years old,[69] was not on the game or my dad. It was everything else around me—the grandstand, the huge stadium, and the people all around, all new to me. Excitement filled me as my little brain raced with thoughts, my head jerking from right to between to left, my grandma uttering those unforgettable loving words: "You're so frisky."

That memory reminds me of the dissimilarities in thoughts between a babe and a mature adult. Their foci are completely on different levels. The infant cannot recognize his father from a distance. Unlike the mature adult, its mind is unable to discern subtle distinctions. In the same way, an immature Christian is distracted and unsophisticated in noting the differences between the real and the substitute, the camouflage, or the counterfeit. For that reason they are easily deceived into believing false teachings and following false teachers. Spiritual growth of Church members remedies spiritual infanthood.

Verse 15: **"Instead, speaking the truth in love, we will grow to become in every respect the mature body of him who is the head, that is, Christ."** The tense here continues to be future. One evidence Paul suggests of those growing towards spiritual maturity is of their "speaking the truth in love." What does that mean? In the context of the previous verse, the activities of deceivers upon the spiritually immature, speaking the truth is the contrast, the activity of the spiritually mature. To do so in love is to obey Jesus' command to his followers. In the context of oneness in maturity, speaking the truth in love is the activity of those who are growing up in Christ. Implied is not only what is spoken but also the source of the words, the mind, as well as the result of the words, the walk in Christ. "Speaking the truth in love" is another way of saying, "talking the talk, walking

---

[69] I surmise my age based on several factors: I wasn't talking in the memory; although I have a brother two years younger than me, my mom did not have a baby on her lap; my grandmother was living with us at the time of my birth but had moved when I was around four or five.

the walk, living the life—of love in Jesus Christ." The future tense of the verbiage identifies the process of growth in mature oneness as ongoing. Jesus, in prayer, seems to have pointed to a time of fulfillment—some time during the lives of those in the third part of his prayer. Paul's echo seems to address an ongoing process during the time of his readership—then and since.

Verse 16: "From him the whole body, joined and held together by every supporting ligament, grows and builds itself up in love, as each part does its work." Everything Paul described in the previous verses rests on the first two words of this sentence: "From him." He, Jesus, initiated the process of growth, and he is its goal. Nonetheless, the growth of the Church includes a role for each Church member, analogous to the roles of individual parts of the human body. Each is part of the whole, and each has a role in its support and togetherness.

Achieving Oneness

Verse 16 is not the conclusion of Paul's message about growth into mature oneness. His next words are, "So, I tell you this" (4:17). What follows are instructions about living as he said in v. 1, "a life worthy of the calling you have received." Reading these instructions forms a portrait of how the Church practicing oneness in spiritual maturity looks.

There is no need to quote the remainder of Ephesians here. Read it if you like, but understand that human effort, regardless of its sincerity or intensity, could never accomplish what Jesus asked the Father to do. Indeed, do your best to practice the instructions, but realize that doing so does not make the Church one. The fact that Jesus prayed for oneness proves that it could not have come about automatically; it was humanly unachievable and inconceivable. As a five-year-old I stood a better chance of erecting our shed alone and by my own ability than Christians, of and by their own effort, stand to succeed in being one and in convincing humanity about God. Nothing that we do can bring it about. Only the power of the almighty, all-knowing, all-wise, all-good Father, Son, and Spirit could bring it about. Yet amazingly, the Triune God has chosen to accomplish it with our participation, granting us the supreme privilege of sharing in the life, joy, and love shared by the Father, Son, and Spirit.

But what about Ecumenism, some may ask? Wouldn't it bring about oneness? Grenz, Guretzki, and Nordling define Ecumenism as: "the attempt to seek a worldwide unity and cooperation among all churches that confess Jesus Christ as Lord."[70] In a sense, ecumenism was a goal of the Church's ancient councils, and in principle, its modern proponents are at least partially in line with Jesus' prayer. Achieving agreement on doctrines and practices, finding common ground without compromise of core beliefs and values would be a wonderful step toward oneness. Where such efforts are underway, my prayer is for success. Nonetheless, Jesus intended more than ecumenism could ever deliver through common doctrines and practices.

Understanding Causes of Division

We have seen that division is the enemy of oneness. Why has the Church been riddled with so much division through its history, and what can 21st Century churches do to "Make every effort to keep the unity of the faith in the bond of peace" (Ephesians 4:3)? To begin to answer these questions, let us consider the Church at Corinth in the mid first century.

On Paul's second missionary journey, he set out from his home base, Antioch, heading west across Asia minor, revisiting cities that he evangelized during his first missionary journey, and finding himself with his entourage crossing the Aegean Sea into southern Europe. After preaching in Macedonia, and planting churches there, he ended up in Greece. Jesus visited him in a vision to encourage him to stay at it in Corinth, the largest city there, reassuring him that the hounding he had taken on his journey had ended, because, as he said, "I have many people in this city" (1 Acts 18:10).

---

[70] Stanley J Grenz, David Guretzki, Cherith Fee Nordling, *Pocket Dictionary of Theological Terms* (Downers Grove, IL., InterVarsity Press, 1999), 43.

Consequently, "Paul stayed for a year and a half, teaching them the word of God" (18:11). There he planted and pastored the congregation in Corinth until he decided to travel back to Judea and on to his home base (18:18, 22). When he began his third missionary journey, he went directly to Ephesus, spending the next two years there, a long way from Corinth. While in Ephesus, he learned about problems that had beset the Corinthian church members, so he penned the first of several letters to them in an effort to resolve them. In 1 Corinthians 1:10, he wrote,

> I appeal to you, brothers and sisters, in the name of our Lord Jesus Christ, that all of you agree with one another in what you say and that there be no divisions among you, but that you be perfectly united in mind and thought.

It was around 53 AD, no more than 20 years after the formation of the Church in Jerusalem, and in Corinth cracks in the oneness Jesus advocated and the Apostles promoted were already showing. The problem was that the members of the church aligned themselves with certain leaders, preferring their styles, personalities, gifts, ideologies, or other distinguishing factors (1:12). Paul asked them a three-worded piercing question that ought to haunt Church members through all time: "Is Christ divided" (1:13)? Paul went on bluntly to label this sectarian tendency spiritual immaturity, writing in 1 Corinthians 3:1-4:

> Brothers and sisters, I could not address you as people who live by the Spirit but as people who are still worldly—mere infants in Christ. I gave you milk, not solid food, for you were not yet ready for it. Indeed, you are still not ready. You are still worldly. For since there is jealousy and quarreling among you, are you not worldly? Are you not acting like mere humans? For when one

says, "I follow Paul," and another, "I follow Apollos," are you not mere human beings?

Blunt, absolutely! Their actions were "worldly" and those of "mere human beings." This was their behavior despite actually being "sanctified in Christ Jesus and called to be his holy people" (1 Corinthians 1:2). It's not that these people were unchristian; simply, they were not living lives worthy of their calling. The New Testament writers did not hide the weaknesses and failures of Church members. As pointed out in Chapter 1 of this book, they were still under construction, being built up, not yet mature, not even close to it! Jesus had said that he had many people in Corinth—a city especially known for its immoral practices. Sadly, at that time, too many of the Corinthian church members were conforming to the world around them—the reason Paul labeled them "worldly."

Here we have insight into the problem with schisms, splits, divisions throughout church history and the issue of church division today. That is why movements such as modern ecumenism will not of themselves solve the problem.

To further sharpen our insight, let's look deeper into the problem at Corinth that led to their division. Looking back at the time of Paul's pastoral service there, Luke explained in Acts 18:18, "Paul stayed on in Corinth for some time. Then he left the brothers and sailed for Syria." Luke adds in 18:24, "Meanwhile a Jew named Apollos, a native of Alexandria..." and in 19:1, "While Apollos was at Corinth...." After Paul's departure, Apollos and others assumed leadership roles in the Corinthian church. The intended roles of these leaders were to build up the church, as Paul wrote: "I laid the foundation as an expert builder and someone else is building on it" (1 Corinthians 3:10). Paul implied that someone had built "wood, hay, or straw" onto the foundation of Jesus Christ (3:11-12). Thus, there was damage from the pulpit that stunted the spiritual growth of the members.

Apollos was one but not the only influential leader, some of whom Paul later called "false apostles, deceitful workmen, masquerading as apostles of Christ" (2 Corinthians 11:13). Who were these men, and more importantly, what were their motives? Paul did not name them but told the church members that they were putting up with a leader who "enslaves you or exploits you or takes advantage of you" (11:20). Combine preachers harboring ulterior motives with a group lacking spiritual maturity and the result is the mess that Paul desperately tried to resolve by writing two letters that became part of the New Testament.

It appears that the Corinthian church had developed cliques that claimed allegiance to human leaders. If we were to give them names today based upon their self designations as followers of individuals then, we might call them Paulatians, Apollosians, Cephans, or Christians (1 Corinthians 1:12). Yes, even the group with the "good" name was part of the problem. It's not the name that they adopt that matters; it's who they **really** are following. Paul urged them to follow Jesus when he wrote, "Follow my example, as I follow the example of Christ" (1 Corinthians 11:1). That is the bottom line. Following Jesus would remedy division.

Turning to Jesus

That may seem like an oversimplification, but is it? If you were lost deep in a jungle, which alternative would provide the best choice for escape: a map, a set of written directions, or an experienced, reputable guide? Perhaps you might not like any of the alternatives, and instead, would prefer to avoid the jungle. The problem is that this world is like a spiritual jungle, and all humanity is lost in it, with no way of escape unless it is through the Guide—Jesus Christ—"for there is no other name under heaven given to men by which we must be saved" (Acts 4:12).

Some churches might reply, "Yes, we have that: Jesus Christ is our Guide and Salvation," even as they take a firm stand on their distinctive beliefs as more correct than others. But is Jesus their guide? How could he be the guide of all when all disagree? Paul did not advise the Corinthian church members to follow whatever group they chose. He didn't even want them to follow him unless he was following Jesus Christ. Most churches might argue, "We are following Jesus Christ," even as they reason that others are not, so please, let's try to be objective: If the Orthodox believe that they have it more right than the Catholics, and the Catholics believe that they have it more right than the Protestants, and the Protestants believe that they have it more right than the cults, and each cult believes that only it has it right, someone is wrong. Objectively, the question for each is, do **we** have it right?

No question, Jesus is right. He said, "I am the way and the truth and the life" (John 14:6). So, as Paul urged, the only right way is to follow Christ. What if every church was willing to undergo an independent examination—a spiritual audit, so to speak—of its theology, its doctrines, and its practices, with the intention of complete conformance to Jesus Christ and commitment to change everything found to be nonconforming?

Unrealistic, perhaps, but not impossible with God. Let us now consider a biblical example of a group that changed its essential beliefs and practices to conform to Jesus Christ. The story begins in Acts 18:24: "Meanwhile a Jew named Apollos, a native of Alexandria, came to Ephesus." This is the same Apollos who later was in Corinth. He arrived in Ephesus, a major city in Asia Minor, shortly after Paul passed through on his way to Judea. Apollos was "a learned man, with a thorough knowledge of the Scriptures," and apparently he worked as an itinerant preacher. His home, Alexandria, a large city on the Mediterranean coast of Egypt, a center of Hellenistic culture and philosophical learning, was residence of a huge Jewish population. Apollos' message, was about the Messiah—Christ— but it was incomplete because "he knew only the baptism of John" (18:25). This message gained followers through the proclamation of the coming of the Messiah and urging of hearers to repent—change their lives to obedience to God—and be baptized, in much the same way that John the Baptist previously had taught (Mark 1:4-8).

Apollos' message might have been considered similar to Paul's, proclaiming the Messiah in Jewish Synagogues and baptizing, so it may have appeared to be like the Christianity that was rapidly spreading in those parts of the Roman Empire. A group of followers emerged in Ephesus. About them, Luke wrote: "While Apollos was at Corinth, Paul took the road through the interior and arrived at Ephesus. There he found some disciples" (Acts 19:1). Paul discovered that these followers had received an incomplete message and told them about Jesus (19:2-4). This group, not interested in holding on to their incomplete beliefs, turned to Jesus, was baptized, received the Holy Spirit, and followed Paul (19:5-7). They turned from making **their** repentance and obedience the center of their practice to faith in **Jesus**, following him as disciples; thereby, they were some of the first of what became the Church at Ephesus.

Perhaps this seems to be too simple an example to apply to a larger group, organized as a church with an established hierarchy of leadership, but is it?

The twentieth century, with its two devastating world wars, the cold war with its threat of nuclear Armageddon, and post-modern declining interest in Christianity in the Western world could hardly be thought of as the scene of a dramatic display of the grace of God and echo of Jesus' prayer. But almost hidden under the rubbish heap of negative church stories is the amazing transformation of an obscure relatively small church considered by many Evangelical Christians to be a cult—the Worldwide Church of God (WCG). About this transformation, Ruth Tucker wrote in 1996: "Never before in the history of Christianity has there been such a complete move to orthodox Christianity by an unorthodox fringe church."[71]

I do not intend here to retell this story, which is well documented in books such as Joseph Tkach's *Transformed by Truth*[72] and J. Michael Feazell's *The Liberation of the Worldwide Church of God*.[73] Instead, I would like to share an inside story, because I was a member of this fringe church that turned to Jesus.

---

[71] Ruth Tucker, *Christianity Today*, "From the Fringe to the Fold", July 15, 1996, 26-27.

[72] Joseph Tkach, , *Transformed By Truth* (Oregon: Multnomah Publishers, 1997).

[73] J. Michael Feazell, *The Liberation of the Worldwide Church of God* (Grand Rapids, MI: Zondervan, 2001).

On December 24, 1994 I was in Big Sandy, Texas to pick up my daughter for a scheduled break from her college studies. She was a student at Ambassador University, which was affiliated with the WCG. While there, I heard WCG President and Pastor General, Joseph W. Tkach, deliver a four-hour sermon about the New Covenant.[74] As an Elder in that church and a passionate baptized Christian for many years, I was familiar with the New Testament teaching about the Old and New Covenants, nonetheless, that sermon, and the text of it that was mailed to all WCG Elders, shook me to the core.

In early January, 1995 as I was reviewing the text, I became emotional. Throwing the legal-sized document to the floor in our family room, I fell to my knees, tears streaming down my face, and said, "Father, if this is true, everything I have believed is wrong! Lord Jesus, please save me, and save the Worldwide Church of God." My prayer was immediately answered; I experienced an unexplainable presence in the room and a quiet calm. I rose, put the Tkach letter in a desk drawer, and opened my Bible to read it again afresh, starting with Acts 15. I concluded this brief study with, "Hmmm, there's something to this." This experience of Jesus was unprecedented. Thirty years had gone by in which I had drifted from a warm interest in Jesus, in those early days of Bible reading, to a strict legalistic approach to God. I still related to the Father, but Jesus was not personal to me. Instead, I had swallowed many conditions to my salvation, such as observance of the seventh-day Sabbath and annual holy days, conditions that I considered essential. From this moment in 1995, I began to feel a new sense of freedom. Over the next few days, figurative scales fell from my eyes as I read through the books of Galatians and Hebrews. I was beginning to understand. But more than simply a change in my viewpoint of Bible

---

[74] Joseph Tkach, 23. "That all changed with a landmark sermon my dad [Tkach, Sr.] gave on Christmas Eve 1994. This is often called 'The New Covenant/Old Covenant' sermon, and it once and for all convinced the skeptics within our own church that the changes were for real and that they were permanent."

scriptures, I was experiencing an inner change that I could not explain, describing them to my friends as changes "not just to my understanding but to me." A revolution in my life was occurring.

This same revolution was spreading like wildfire throughout the Worldwide Church of God. Members of the local congregation I attended and served, as well as most of my personal friends in the church, were dazed at the startling change that the leadership of the WCG had made and was actively, aggressively, and fearlessly teaching. Our worship services and other meetings underwent striking changes in effort to center everything in the grace of God through Jesus Christ. The change was more than some could handle, so large numbers left, most of them becoming members of new groups that sprung up to hold on to the former teachings. Throughout our worldwide fellowship of congregations, the consequences were felt in decreased donations and lower church attendance. Despite these effects, the church leadership was undaunted, and so were those of us who followed. We suffered deep emotional pain over the departures of many people that we loved; some even experienced fractures in family relationships. Nonetheless, together we considered ourselves on a great spiritual journey. Everything was up for review: doctrine, theology, traditions, procedures, and practices. Humbly obedient, we were willing to throw off everything that distracts from Jesus; we were willing to change anything where we were shown to be wrong; we endeavored to treat ministers of Christ as "servants" (1 Corinthians 3:5; 4:6), not getting caught up in one's charisma.

Twenty years since, we are small among denominations, now known as Grace Communion International, still on a marvelous journey, and slowly growing again![75]

---

[75] The mention of the example of Grace Communion International is not an attempt to induce anyone to join that church. Rather, it is encouragement to other churches to consider the example of a church that turned to Jesus at the expense of financial loss. My prayer is that this book encourages the Church—in its many diverse groups—toward oneness, not further division and sectarianism.

Abiding in Jesus

With many churches, changing to conform to Jesus will not be as extensive as it was for the Worldwide Church of God. But any change in response to the Holy Spirit's initiative to conform to Jesus will be radical. In some cases, the change may come in the form of slight doctrinal or theological corrections to restore what has over time slipped into error from Christian orthodoxy.

Again, the New Testament includes a real story of restoration of Christ-centered beliefs and practices in churches that had strayed. The churches in the province of Galatia were early results of the evangelistic preaching of Paul and Barnabas during their first missionary journey. Luke described the evangelization of residents of the province in Acts 13:32, "We tell you the good news: What God promised our ancestors he has fulfilled for us, their children, by raising up Jesus." The speaker continued as Luke added, in 13:38,

> Therefore, my friends, I want you to know that through Jesus the forgiveness of sins is proclaimed to you. Through him everyone who believes is set free from every sin, a justification you were not able to obtain under the law of Moses.

The message resonated with many Synagogue attendees, aware of their spiritual need and seeking answers. Consequently, "The word of the Lord spread through the whole region" (13:49). This Gospel message was Christ-centered, announcing his resurrection, proclaiming the forgiveness of sins through him, and assuring that freedom through Jesus achieved what the Law of Moses could not. Jews and Gentiles flocked to the new churches set up in the province.

Strangely, after such a remarkable start, some of these same churches reoriented themselves to religious beliefs and activities centered on themselves and their acts of religious piety. They became churches that strayed from the Gospel of the grace of

God through Jesus Christ to a false gospel that emphasized obedience to law as the central thrust of their Christian religion. Paul, passionately stirred to convince the church members of their errors and to turn them back to Jesus, wrote these challenging words that we can read in Galatians 1:6-7:

> I am astonished that you are so quickly deserting the one who called you to live in the grace of Christ and are turning to a different gospel— which is really no gospel at all. Evidently some people are throwing you into confusion and are trying to pervert the gospel of Christ.

These church members had embraced ideas that spawned beliefs and practices different from the Church that Paul called the Body of Christ, the Church that had started in Jerusalem, spread to cities throughout Judea, Samaria, and Syria. They had moved away from the Apostolically-established orthodoxy of the Church, establishing their own distinctive views. Paul continued in Galatians 3:1-3:

> You foolish Galatians! Who has bewitched you? Before your very eyes Jesus Christ was clearly portrayed as crucified. I would like to learn just one thing from you: Did you receive the Spirit by the works of the law, or by believing what you heard? Are you so foolish? After beginning by means of the Spirit, are you now trying to finish by means of the flesh?

The problem with the religion of the churches in Galatia was that instead of being Christ-centered and Spirit-led it was law-oriented and self-initiated. Paul regarded this as such a problem that he wrote in Galatians 5:1-6:

It is for freedom that Christ has set us free. Stand firm, then, and do not let yourselves be burdened again by a yoke of slavery. Mark my words! I, Paul, tell you that if you let yourselves be circumcised, Christ will be of no value to you at all. Again I declare to every man who lets himself be circumcised that he is obligated to obey the whole law. You who are trying to be justified by the law have been alienated from Christ; you have fallen away from grace. For through the Spirit we eagerly await by faith the righteousness for which we hope. For in Christ Jesus neither circumcision nor uncircumcision has any value. The only thing that counts is faith expressing itself through love.

The result of their "Christian" legalism was that they became "alienated from Christ" and "fallen away from grace." Unless change took place, these churches were headed toward separation from Jesus, the Vine (John 15:6), causing them to "wither" spiritually. Paul called on them to return to Jesus Christ as the center of their beliefs and practice.

The New Testament says little about the outcome of Paul's attempt to restore the churches in Galatia, and the absence of detail is itself informative. If these churches had either continued their direction or become even more misdirected, Paul's involvement with them would have been a direct response that does not show up in the story written by Luke in the book of Acts. Instead, Luke wrote that when Paul undertook his third missionary journey, he "traveled from place to place throughout the region of Galatia and Phrygia, strengthening all of the disciples" (Acts 18:23). To strengthen them, he must have been successful in restoring them to beliefs and practices based on the grace of Jesus Christ.

The biblical story of the churches in Galatia illustrates the Holy Spirit's intention to lead any and all who have fallen into similar errors to turn to Jesus and enjoy the freedom, truth, and oneness that ensues.

James B. Torrance commented on modern churches that need this turn to Jesus: "There is no more urgent need in our churches today than to recover the Trinitarian nature of grace— that it is by grace alone, through the gift of Jesus Christ in the Spirit that we can enter into and live a life of communion with God our Father."[76] Torrance summarized the pitfalls of a false understanding of God and of legalism:

> The counterpart of seeing God as a sovereign individual Monad "out there" is a very individualistic concept of worship... The counterpart of a legalistic concept of God as the contract-God who rewards human merit is certain medieval doctrines of penance... or false notions of the mass as a propitiatory sacrifice. It can also lead to the notion of a Protestant work ethic; a false activism, emphasis on prosperity as a motive for Christian giving or tithing, or setting criteria for evaluation of success in churches and their ministries. It can blend with certain forms of revivalism.[77]

These erroneous notions, doctrines and practices of many churches today, are countered by a sweeping return to Jesus, considering his love-relationship with the Father, remembering their self-sacrificing love for all humanity, responding to grace with trust, recalling Jesus' prayer that his followers are one as he and the Father are one, and endeavoring to keep the oneness of the Spirit in the bond of peace. Those who seek to follow Jesus,

---

[76] James B Torrance, *Worship, Community and the Triune God of Grace* (Downers Grove, IL: InterVarsity Press, 1996), 59.

[77] James B Torrance, 72.

regardless of their affiliation, will find themselves standing together at Jesus' feet. They will recognize their diversity, but always they will emphasize their commonality—their oneness in Christ. Uppermost in their minds will be the loving acceptance they enjoy in their relationship with the Father, Son, and Spirit; this relationship will spur them to so accept and love one another.

Of course, such a radical turnabout in churches has not occurred in history. To write about it here is to look forward to the echo of Jesus' prayer and its effect on the Church. Even as I write, there are ripples of this echo appearing and spreading. A case in point is the emergence in the 20th Century of Neo-Orthodoxy in Europe, progressing toward Trinitarian theology compatible with the Orthodox teaching of the early Greek Church fathers, and spreading among certain Protestant denominations. From a theological perspective, this trend moves East and West closer to each other. As this movement continues to progress, and more scholars, authors, pastors, and especially churches are moved to embrace it, the Church will increasingly move toward its intended center—Jesus Christ—along with his revelation of the divine love relationship in God the Father through the Holy Spirit and including all of Jesus' followers. **Finding themselves in union with the triune God through Christ, these churches will, in a sense, look around and notice each other at Jesus' feet, sparking in them the question, why remain divided**?

Dismantling Divisive Walls

Although human effort will not bring about the oneness of Jesus' prayer, individuals and churches can take steps to remove barriers they erected to this oneness.

The Church in the first-century excelled at being inclusive, accepting as members people of all nations, races, and economic classes; gender, age, and health condition were never factors. Paul summed up this practice in Galatians 3:28: "There is neither Jew nor Gentile, neither slave nor free, nor is there male and female, for you are all one in Christ Jesus." Two thousand years later, the nations, cultures, and institutions of this world still struggle with inclusion. They can learn much from the standard established by Jesus and explained by Paul in Ephesians 2:14-18:

> For he himself is our peace, who has made the two groups one and has destroyed the barrier, the dividing wall of hostility, by setting aside in his flesh the law with its commands and regulations. His purpose was to create in himself one new humanity out of the two, thus making peace, and in one body to reconcile both of them to God through the cross, by which he put to death their hostility. He came and preached peace to you who were far away and peace to those who were near. For through him we both have access to the Father by one Spirit.

Jesus tore down the ancient wall that divided Jews and Gentiles. Through the covenant at Mt. Sinai, God had established the Israelites as his people and himself as their God, differentiating them from the rest of the world's peoples. This covenant, to safeguard Israel from paganism, temporarily separated Israelites from other nations, but its ultimate aim was to bring them together in the worship of the one true God. At the establishment of the covenant, God explained to Moses its intent, and Moses wrote about it in Exodus 19:3-6:

> This is what you are to say to the descendants of Jacob and what you are to tell the people of Israel: 'You yourselves have seen what I did to Egypt, and how I carried you on eagles' wings and brought you to myself. Now if you obey me fully and keep my covenant, then out of all nations you will be my treasured possession. Although the whole earth is mine, you will be for me a kingdom of priests and a holy nation.'

Israel was to become a kingdom of priests, serving God among the nations. God made clear that the whole earth belonged to him, including every nation, but among these Israel was to be a holy nation. Just as in Israel's temple worship God used priests as his servants to mediate between him and humans, he intended to do the same with all humanity through the nation of Israel. Sadly, the Israelites misunderstood their God-intended role, thinking of this covenant and its Law as God's way to separate humanity and designate them as superior. Jews in Jesus' day retained this misconception that Jesus corrected through the establishment of the New Covenant (Hebrews 8:13).

The Church is the Israel of the New Covenant (Galatians 6:16). That is why Paul could write that "If you belong to Christ, then you are Abraham's seed, and heirs according to the promise" (Galatians 3:29). But from its beginning in the first century, the Church has struggled with this concept, first in the Jew-Gentile relationship, later on a large scale the East-West relationship. In the United States, the Gospel spawned new churches across the expanding territories, but racially they have never been integrated. Instead of embracing the oneness established by Jesus and bonded by the Holy Spirit, many churches adopted the same misconception held by the Israelites, thereby constructing new walls.

But Jesus has always been a step ahead. He anticipated the difficulty the Church would have in keeping the oneness of the Spirit, so he prayed to the Father for the Church. In response, every church needs to consider the barriers and walls around them that hinder them from being one with others in Christ.

Division turned the beautiful picture of the first-century Church into a jigsaw puzzle of pieces, hopelessly alienated from each other like the same poles of a magnet. The Church is to be the light of the world, and the world desperately needs an example of unity. Consider the results of division in the previous century: racial oppression and strife in "civilized" countries, WWI, WWII, the Cold War, and genocide in Africa, Asia, and Europe. The oneness of Jesus is the solution to these otherwise irresolvable problems. Division among peoples of different cultures, races, religions exists because of a lack of a perceptible common bond. Instead of oneness, the ideologies of the groups—fed by religious misconceptions—divide them with notions of superiority, rightness of selves, and wrongness of others, and as it is in the world so has it been in the Church.

Jesus destroyed all barriers and brought all together with the common bonds of the same Father, the same Lord, the same Spirit dwelling in all, common baptism, shared hope and faith (Ephesians 4:4-6). When his followers accept his grace and obey his command to love one another, they have no basis for remaining divided. When Jesus' followers take up their cross to follow him, they imitate his demolition of divisive walls (Ephesians 2:14-16; Matthew 16:24).

Can the Church rediscover the value of councils as a means of encouraging and strengthening oneness? One of my professors, Dr. Dan Rogers of Grace Communion Seminary, once commented: "Also instructive is the process Luke lays out in Acts 15 for resolving the greatest divisive controversy in the history of the Church. It may be viewed as a paradigm for the Church striving for oneness. And that paradigm can be incredibly useful in dealing with disagreements/divisions in a local congregation (or in a denomination): 1) disagreement 2) open discussion 3) discerning God's will 4) responding to God's will 5) participating with God in his will through action steps resulting in unity/consensus."

The piece-by-piece demolition of divisive walls between local churches, inspired by the love of God, expressed in the grace of Christ, and humbly responded to in members, churches, and denominations will echo Jesus prayer in its participants and beyond, perhaps stirring those largest segments of the Church to consider their walls of division.

Oneness is a property of the Trinity and the emphasis of Jesus' prayer; as such it is non-negotiable. Dear fellow followers of Jesus Christ, whoever and wherever we are, it is utterly unacceptable for the Church to remain divided. To continue to conform to the world defies the Church's identity of belonging to Jesus Christ. Therefore let all of us join Jesus in praying to the Father that we may be one!

The Effect of Oneness on the World

Twice in John 17, Jesus spoke of the world being affected by the oneness of His followers. He said "so that the world may believe that you have sent me" (21) and "to let the world know that you sent me" (23). Both of these statements were made in the third part of the prayer—the part for the followers of Jesus after the apostles. What is the significance of these requests? Why did Jesus say nothing about the world believing or knowing in the second part—the part for the Twelve and his followers with him then?

I do not intend to suggest an answer to these questions. These words of Jesus, as many others, could have eschatological—age to come—implications.[78] Jesus did not say when the world would believe and know. I consider the *when* of these questions beyond explanation unless or until Jesus reveals the answer. However, because Jesus specified in prayer that the world would believe and know that he was truly sent by the Father, it is unquestionable that His prayer will be answered, and Jesus has already revealed how. Johnson and Webber explain:

> The fundamental character mark is to be the divine love-in-fellowship. The decisive mark of the Father is the love by which he gives all things to the Son (v. 7); that of the Son is in his yielding all glory back to the Father. This is a relationship of total and mutual self-giving. Christ's people will demonstrate that they are his people by exhibiting this kind of love. As they self-

---

[78] Thomas F. Torrance, *Royal Priesthood* (New York, NY: T&T Clark, 1995), 43.

sacrificially serve one another, the presence of
Christ will be made visible to the world (v. 21).[79]

The idea is astonishing! Advertisers dream of ways to get
attention that put their clients' products in view of potential
customers. Those who post their videos on YouTube seek to
have them go viral. Jesus said, "By this everyone will know that
you are my disciples, if you love one another" (John 13:35). The
perfect tool of evangelism to reach the world is the love of God,
poured out upon humanity through Jesus Christ, expressed in the
Church through the Holy Spirit, radiating this love from human
heart to human heart of each Church member, witnessed by a
hostile world.

God the Father did not send His Son into the world in vain!
"But that the world through him might be saved" (John 3:16).
Jesus' prayer for the Church has implications for the world. Let's
consider these implications. If "everyone will know" that the
followers of Jesus truly love one another, a spectacular fact is on
display before their eyes: an unprecedented, inconceivable, and
impossible ideal actually playing out in a group of human beings!
Never before has such a thing happened. The story of Jesus…
proven to be true by his followers!

Although noticed, paradoxically, this spectacle may not
immediately be appreciated. The world did not accept Jesus, and
he said of his followers, "they are not of the world any more than
I am of the world" (John 17:14). Initially, the opposition likely
will be strong and persecution wide spread, but as many in
Jerusalem, Judea, and Galilee at first opposed Jesus but later
became followers and Church members, so many opposers and
nonbelievers will be won over by the love of Jesus manifested in,
and flowing from, the Church. Paul anticipated such an overflow
of love in one place that he served, and he wrote about it in 1
Thessalonians 3:12, "May the Lord make your love increase and
overflow for each other and for everyone else, just as ours does

---

[79] Johnson and Webber, 331.

for you." As the Father so loved the world that he sent his Son, and Jesus' crucifixion inevitably draws all people, so the Spirit of God, ever making this love increase in Church members toward each other, does not limit it to the Church but causes it to overflow to everyone. Such persistent love, as little-by-little it is perceived, will be difficult to resist, as critics become quiet, and increasing numbers of people realize that an extraordinary phenomenon is emerging before their eyes. Instead of feeling snubbed, judged, and condemned by the Church, they will feel accepted, appreciated, and included. As the Church resembles Jesus, the connection will not escape notice, whether or not what is seen is accepted or rejected.

Since humans transgressed in the Garden of Eden, the human race has not trusted its Creator. Adam and Eve hid because of guilt and fear (Genesis 3:8). In spite of the love they had witnessed in everything done with and for them, they were tainted by the lie, cleverly crafted by the devil, accusing God of not being honest with them and holding back their potential (Genesis 3:4). As humanity spread across the earth, and invented gods to worship, they superimposed their own dishonesty, selfishness, mean-spirit, hateful, anger-prone, unforgiving, and unloving character on their gods. They feared them but could not love them, and they manifested their fear and hostility toward the one true God when he was revealed to them. Only the truth about God—"the compassionate and gracious God, slow to anger, abounding in love and faithfulness, maintaining love to thousands, and forgiving wickedness, rebellion and sin" (Exodus 34:6-7)—could change the deceived, confused, and biased human mind. Jesus, on behalf of the Father and the Spirit, convincingly demonstrated the love and grace of God, but the decision was made in heaven to complete the project—the world coming to believe and know—through the participation of Jesus' followers.

If we take Jesus' words seriously, the love of the Father for the Son and the Son for the Father—both through the Holy Spirit—include love for Jesus' followers, who love each other and overflow with love for all humanity. This love will bring to the world belief, and when perfected, knowledge of **who is** the one true God and what the Trinity has done (John 17:21, 23).

My dad lovingly invited me to participate in his work project, and through my childlike love for him that valued being part of his life and activities—a human-type of oneness—I participated in helping to build his shed. Similarly, the Father invites us to participate in oneness with him, in Jesus and through the Holy Spirit, in helping to build His building! What a privilege! Jesus prayed and may the Church echo his prayer. As Carol Cymbala, in her beautiful contemporary song, *Make Us One* puts it,

Make us one, Lord,
Make us one,
Holy Spirit, make us one.
Let Your love flow
So the world will know
We are one in You.

Conclusion

Jesus prayed for oneness in the Church, so what should the Church do? This is the natural question to ask, but before there is an effort to start a movement, it is essential to remind ourselves that what humans **do** is not the work of God; Jesus prayed that the **Father** would work in his followers through the Holy Spirit. The simple answer is, obey Jesus. He said, "A new command I give you: Love one another. As I have loved you, so you must love one another" (John 13:34). Jesus' love involved self sacrifice— laying down his life; he calls on his followers to do the same, in most cases not as martyrs, but as Paul elaborated, "as living sacrifices" (Romans 12:1). To keep this command, one must first keep the prerequisite—to trust Jesus; otherwise, there would be no basis for obeying his command. John explained as follows in 1 John 3:23: "And this is his command: to believe in the name of his Son, Jesus Christ, and to love one another as he commanded us."

There are many other **dos** with examples that could be mentioned to encourage churches to apply oneness, but I think that we should stop here and, as Carol Cymbala so beautifully composed, defer to the Holy Spirit to do his work, sweeping Jesus' followers up in love and thrusting them forward in mission.

Finally, as the Church waits for the full and complete answer to Jesus' prayer, regardless of how long it takes, even if it is until Christ returns, it is appropriate, important, and essential that Jesus' followers pray for its fulfillment. As they pray what Jesus prayed, they participate in echoing his prayer, and as those prayers are answered, the impossible becomes real.

Now, let us return to the story of my dad building the shed. He called me and I came. He told me to hold the board, and I reached out and grabbed it. With his urging, I held it with all my might. But I had no inner strength to accomplish the task of holding the board. Therefore, I could not take responsibility for the project's success. Nor could I initiate the work of building the shed. If I had embarked upon the project when my daddy was not there, I might have expended effort, but nothing would have been accomplished, and most likely something would have been damaged. Throughout the project I had to participate—remain in oneness—with my daddy. It is exactly the same with the Church. The Father calls individuals to loving relationships, in his Son, through his Spirit, and with each other, putting these individuals together into one Body, the Church, giving it a task beyond its ability. The Church responds in trust and continues in oneness with the Father through Jesus in the Holy Spirit.

When my dad charged me to hold the board—the board that in fact he was fully holding, he caused my grip to echo his charge. He drew me into his plan and activity so that I became an eager and willing participant in an accomplishment way beyond my ability, one that only he could accomplish. In so doing, he made me part of himself, sharing with me the joy that he had in our relationship.

An echo is merely the reflection of power from its source. When one stands on a cliff and shouts so that the waves produced by a voice bounce off the nearby hillsides, it is not the hillsides that produce the sound, it is the voice. In the same way, Jesus' prayer to the Father results in the power of oneness from the Father to reverberate, so to speak, in the Church in such a way that the result is an echo. This echo is so powerful that it will vibrate, so to speak, the world itself, and the outcome is that the world—the human race—is convinced of God the Father and Jesus Christ the Son, convinced of their loving relationship, convinced that their relationship includes and envelopes the Church, and thereby alerted that it all extends to the rest of Creation.

Thanks to our loving Lord who prayed this marvelous prayer for us! Thanks to our loving Father who answers Jesus' prayer through the Holy Spirit, transforming the Church! May we, members of the Body of Christ in all of its diversity worldwide, believe, that is, trust in the One who is trustworthy, who faithfully answers prayer, keeps his promises, and brings his wonderful will to pass. Amen.

Appendix

Athanasius Writes about Oneness

Athanasius, fourth century Bishop of the Alexandria Church, served as one of the most notable contributors to the oneness of the Church through his input to, and defense of, the Nicene-Constantinopolitan Creed. Although he did not live to see this creed established in 381 AD, his ministry through much of his adult lifetime countered the false teaching of the Arians that denied Jesus' divinity, and gave the Church steady sound teaching that retained the message of the apostles about Jesus. In the process, Athanasius' prolific written apologetics, translated into English, give much insight into the understanding of the early Church. In defense of Jesus' deity and explanation of the oneness of the Church members with the Trinity, he wrote the following:

> And, as has been said, by so becoming one, as the Father and the Son, we shall be such, not as the Father is by nature in the Son and the Son in the Father, but according to our own nature, and as it is possible for us thence to be moulded and to learn how we ought to be one, just as we learned also to be merciful. For like things are naturally one with like; thus all flesh is ranked together in kind; but the Word is unlike us and like the Father. And therefore, while He is in nature and truth one with His own Father, we, as being of one kind with each other (for from one were all made, and one is the nature of all men), become one with each other in good disposition, having as our copy the Son's natural unity with the Father. For as He taught us meekness from

Himself, saying, 'Learn of Me for I am meek and lowly in heart,' not that we may become equal to Him, which is impossible, but that looking towards Him, we may remain meek continually, so also here wishing that our good disposition towards each other should be true and firm and indissoluble, from Himself taking the pattern, He says, 'that they may be one as We are,' whose oneness is indivisible; that is, that they learning from us of that indivisible Nature, may preserve in like manner agreement one with another. And this imitation of natural conditions is especially safe for man, as has been said; for, since they remain and never change, whereas the conduct of men is very changeable, one may look to what is unchangeable by nature, and avoid what is bad and remodel himself on what is best.[80]

Michael Jenkins Writes about Oneness

Michael Jinkins' *Invitation to Theology,* organized around the Apostles Creed, addresses the subject of union with the Trinity through Jesus Christ under the topic "The Holy Catholic Church." [81] There, Jinkins emphasizes that the Universal Church has been, from the beginning, the integration of humans into communion with the triune God.[82] "At the heart of our identity as the Church of Jesus Christ lives the reality of our spiritual union with Christ."[83] The Church is not a social institution. It is more than a place for the companionship of those with like minds. Church unity is not the same as unanimity. In Christ diversity is normal and essential. The unity is in him through the Holy Spirit.

---

[80] Athanasius, *Select Works and Letters* (Discourse III, 20 nfnf204.pdf). *Nicene and Post Nicene Fathers* Series 2, Vol.4, Philip Schaff, ed.

[81] Michael Jinkins, *Invitation to Theology* (Downers Grove, IL: InterVarsity Press, 2001).

[82] Jinkins, 214-215.

[83] Ibid., 217.

Jenkins views the concepts of solitary and voluntary Christians as part of a myth about the Church. Because the Church consists of humans being made into the "spitting-image" of Jesus, the process is messy at best.[84] This explains the importance of oneness, expanded by Jinkins to include *koinonia*, that is, participation in the communion of Father, Son, and Spirit; *diakonia*, service (or ministry) in Jesus' authority in the same way that he serves; and *leitourgia* (literally, the work of the people), worship in the total life of the Church saying Amen to everything of the Father, Son, and Spirit.[85]

Together 2016 – a Trend Toward Oneness?

On July 16, 2016 in Washington, DC the largest gathering of Christians of different denominations in United States history assembled on the National Mall for prayer, praise/worship singing, and preaching.

A large gathering of Evangelicals the day before the start of the Republican National Convention might seem to have been driven by a political motive, but according to its organizers this event had only Jesus as its agenda, and its attendees included members of many Christian denominations and communions— Protestants and Catholics.

Summarizing this event, Wade Heath of *The Blaze* wrote:

> The concept is this: one million young people gather together on the National Mall in Washington, D.C. to humble themselves before Jesus and unite in prayer to ask for a reset on our country and on our life. No one specific denomination, no church; just the Holy Spirit, the power of love and the desire to change things for the better.[86]

---

[84] Ibid., 225.

[85] Ibid., 226-229.

[86] Wade Heath, *The Blaze*, "Can A Millennial Faith Revival Reset America?", July 14,

I, along with my wife, our daughter and son-in-law, and their three children, attended, and I found it deeply inspiring to experience the spirit of inclusion, love, and Christian unity inside the fence around the National Mall in face of the outside division and hatred so rampant in the nation. The tone was one of unity and inclusion of all in Christ.

Also known as Jesus Reset, the event organizers targeted Millennials, a group that was strongly represented in the attendance; however, thousands spanning the generations from pre-teens to senior citizens also were there. Quoting Nick Hall, the event organizer, Heath continued:

> This is really our effort to say what if we all came together for one day, for one purpose, to lift up Jesus, to get outside of the norm as this isn't about any one group or one denomination or

2016, http://www.theblaze.com/contributions/can-a-millennial-revival-reset-america/

church, but this is about all of us gathering together under the banner of Jesus and praying that he would move in our hearts and move in our nation.

Several things about this event grab my attention, leading me to include it in this Appendix: First, everything is centered in Jesus; second, an absence of sectarianism; third, a spirit of love and inclusion; fourth, heavy participation of young people. I wonder: if the thrust of this event continues, could it become part of a movement that signals a third Great Awakening in the United States—an awakening that crosses denominational lines and draws Jesus' followers together? I hope and pray that it is; the need is so great!

Sources

Anyabwile, Thabiti M. *The Decline of African American Theology.* Downers Grove, IL: InterVarsity Press, 2007.

Athanasius, *Select Works and Letters.* (Discourse III, 20 nfnf204.pdf). *Nicene and Post Nicene Fathers* Series 2, Vol.4, Philip Schaff, ed.

Blum, E. A. *The Bible Knowledge Commentary: An Exposition of the Scriptures "John".* Wheaton, IL: Victor Books, 1985.

Brown, Raymond E., Joseph A. Fitzmyer, Roland E. Murphy. *The New Jerome Biblical Commentary.* Englewood Cliffs, NJ: Prentice-Hall, 1990.

Carson, D. A., R. T. Fance, J. A. Motyer, G. J. Wenhan. *New Bible Commentary.* Downers Grove, IL: InterVarsity Press, 1994.

Eusebius. *The Church History of Eusebius,* X.III.1. *Nicene and Post Nicene Fathers Series 2, Vol.1*, Philip Schaff, ed. *Grand Rapids, MI: Christian Classics Ethereal Library, 1885*

Feazell, J. Michael. *The Liberation of the Worldwide Church of God.* Grand Rapids, MI: Zondervan, 2001.

Ferm, Vergilius ed. *The Encyclopedia of Religion.* Secaucus, NJ: Poplar Book, 1945.

Gallagher, Robert L. and Paul Hertig eds. *Mission in Acts.* Maryknoll, NY:Orbis Books, 2006.

Grenz, Stanley J, David Guretzki, Cherith Fee Nordling. *Pocket Dictionary of Theological Terms.* Downers Grove, IL., InterVarsity Press, 1999.

Group, Barna. *Americans Divided on the Importance of Church.* March

2014, Barna Group. The Importance of Church.pdf.

Gonzalez, Justo L. *The Story of Christianity Volume 1*. New York, NY: HarperCollins e-books, 1984.

Gorman, Michael J. *Reading Paul*. Eugene, OR: Cascade Books, 2008.

Heath, Wade. *The Blaze.* "Can a Millennial Faith Revival Reset America?" (July 14, 2016) http://www.theblaze.com/contributions/can-a-millennial-revival-reset-america/

Ignatius. Ephesians V, Magnesians III, Trallians II, Philadelphians II, Philip Schaff, ed., *The Apostolic Fathers with Justin Martyr and Irenaeus,* III.1.1 *Ante-Nicene Fathers Vol. 1*. Grand Rapids, MI: Christian Classics Ethereal Library, 1885

Irenaeus. *Against Heresies*, III.1.1 from *Ante-Nicene Fathers Vol. 1*. Philip Schaff, ed. Grand Rapids, MI: Christian Classics Ethereal Library, 1885.

Jamieson, R., A. R. Fausset, & D. Brown. *Commentary Critical and Explanatory on the Whole Bible*. Oak Harbor, WA: Logos Research Systems, Inc., 1997.

Jeffers, James S. *The Greco-Roman World of the New Testament Era*. Downers Grove, IL: InterVarsity Press, 1999.

Jenson, Robert W. *Canon and Creed.* Louisville, KY: Westminster John Knox Press, 2010.

Jinkins, Michael. *Invitation to Theology*. Downers Grove, IL: InterVarsity Press, 2001.

Johnson, Alan F. and Robert E. Webber. *What Christians Believe*. Grand Rapids, MI: Zondervan, 1993.

Lewis, C S. *The Lion, the Witch and the Wardrobe.* Great Brittain, 1950.

Longman, Tremper III and David E. Garland. *The Expositors Bible Commentary: Luke-Acts.* Grand Rapids, MI: Zondervan, 2006.

Longman, Tremper III and David E. Garland. *The Expositors Bible Commentary: Hebrews – Revelation.* Grand Rapids, MI: Zondervan, 2006.

Manuel, Martin S. *Dear Jason.* 2013. available at Amazon.com

Marshall, I. Howard. *New Testament Theology.* Downers Grove, IL: InterVarsity Press, 2004.

McGrath, Alister E. *Christian Theology and Introduction.* Malden, MA: Blackwell Publishers, 1994.

Moloney, Frances J. *Love in the Gospel of John.* Grand Rapids, MI: Baker Academic, 2013.

Mounce, Robert H. *The Expositor's Bible Commentary Revised Edition "John".* Grand Rapids, MI: Zondervan, 2006.

Robertson, Archibald T. *Word Pictures in the New Testament.* Nashville, TN: Broadman Press, 1933. Logos Software 4

Seamands, Stephen. *Ministry in the Image of God.* Downers Grove, IL: InterVarsity Press, 2005.

Smith, Samuel. *Megachurches Seeing Drop in Weekly Attendance, Study Finds.* Christian Post, December 3, 2015.

Spickard, Paul R. and Kevin M. Cragg. *A Global History of Christianity.* Grand Rapids, MI: Baker Academic, 1994.

Stetzer, Ed. *No, American Christianity is not dead.* CNN, May 16, 2015.

Torrance, James B. *Worship, Community and the Triune God of Grace.* Downers Grove, IL: InterVarsity Press, 1996.

Torrance, Thomas F. *Royal Priesthood.* New York, NY: T&T Clark, 1995.

Tucker, Ruth. *Christianity Today*, "From the Fringe to the Fold", July 15, 1996.

Tkach, Joseph. *Transformed By Truth.* Oregon: Multnomah Publishers, 1997.

Volf, Miraslav. *After Our Likeness.* Grand Rapids, MI: Wm. B. Erdmans Publishing, 1998.

Wikipedia. *Religion.* August 2014   http://en.wikipedia.org/wiki/Religion

Wright, Tom. *John for Everyone, Part 2: Chapters 11-21.* Great Brittain: Society Christian Knowledge, 2002.

Young, Frances M. *The Making of the Creeds.* London: SCM Press, 1991.